SIMON GRAY

Simon Gray is the author of over thirty plays and screenplays, including *Butley*, *Otherwise Engaged*, *Close of Play*, *Quartermaine's Terms*, *The Common Pursuit* and *The Late Middle Classes*. He has also written four books about the theatre: *An Unnatural Pursuit*, *How's That For Telling 'em, Fat Lady?*, *Fat Chance* and, most recently, *Enter a Fox*.

By the same author

Plays for the stage

Wise Child
Molly
Spoiled
Dutch Uncle
The Idiot
Butley
Otherwise Engaged
Dog Days
The Rear Column
Close of Play
Stage Struck
Quartermaine's Terms
The Common Pursuit
Melon
Hidden Laughter
The Holy Terror
Cell Mates
Simply Disconnected
Life Support
Just the Three of Us
The Late Middle Classes

Books about the stage

An Unnatural Pursuit
How's That for Telling 'em Fat Lady?
Fat Chance

Simon Gray

JAPES

NICK HERN BOOKS
London
www.nickhernbooks.co.uk

A Nick Hern Book

Japes first published in Great Britain in 2000 as a paperback original by Nick Hern Books Limited, 14 Larden Road, London W3 7ST

Revised reprint 2001

Front cover: August Sander, *Farm Workers*, 1914
© August Sander Archive/SK Stiftung Kultur, 1994;
Man Ray, *Nude*, 1929. Metropolitan Museum of Modern Art, New York. Gift of James Thrall Sobie

Lines on p. 3 from 'Sunday Morning', in *Collected Poems* by Wallace Stevens (Faber & Faber Ltd), quoted with permission of the publisher and Laurence Pollinger

Lines on p. 61 from 'Prufrock and Other Observations', in *Collected Poems 1909-1962* by T.S. Eliot (Faber & Faber Ltd), quoted with permission of the publisher

Lines on p. 58 from 'Missing Dates', in *Collected Poems* by William Empson, originally published by Chatto and Windus, reprinted and quoted by permission of the Random House Group Ltd and Curtis Brown

Typeset by Country Setting, Kingsdown, Kent CT14 8ES
Printed & bound by Antony Rowe Ltd, Eastbourne
ISBN 1 85459 632 2

A CIP catalogue record for this book is available from the British Library

For Piers

26 May 1947–28 June 1996

Japes was first presented at the Mercury Theatre Colchester on 23 November 2000, and subsequently transferred to the Theatre Royal, Haymarket, opening on 7 February 2001. The cast was as follows:

JASON	Toby Stephens
MICHAEL	Jasper Britton
ANITA / WENDY	Clare Swinburne

Director Peter Hall
Designer John Gunter
Lighting Designer Neil Austin

Characters

MICHAEL

WENDY

JASON

ANITA

ACT ONE

Scene One

Early seventies. Sitting room of family house in Hampstead. The house belongs to MICHAEL *and* JASON CARTTS, *brothers.* MICHAEL *is in his mid-twenties,* JASON *a year or so younger.*

Upstage left, door leading off sitting room to other rooms. Kitchen also off stage left.

Sound of typewriter from upstairs.

JASON *is sprawled on sofa in sitting room. He has a bottle of wine beside him, a glass in his hand.*

Sound of typing stops. Footsteps on stairs. MICHAEL *enters sitting room, walks irritably about, ignored by* JASON, *goes out again. Footsteps on stairs. A pause.* MICHAEL *comes back into sitting room, collapses onto chair tensely.*

JASON (*after a pause, mumbles*). Hi.

MICHAEL. Hi. (*Glances at* JASON.) Are you asleep?

JASON. No. I'm trying to remember.

MICHAEL. Remember what?

JASON. 'Sunday Morning'. The last bit. The deer.

MICHAEL. And can you?

JASON. Mmm –
Deer walk upon our mountains, and the quail
Whistles about us their spontaneous cries;
Sweet berries ripen in the wilderness;
And, in the isolation of the sky,
At evening, casual flocks of pigeons make
Ambiguous undulations as they sink,
Downward to darkness, on intended wings.

MICHAEL. 'Extended wings'.

JASON. Yes.

MICHAEL. You said 'intended'. 'Intended wings' – casual flocks of pigeons make / Ambiguous undulations as they sink / Downward to darkness on extended wings. 'Downward to darkness, on intended wings' was your version.

JASON. Are you sure?

MICHAEL. Yes.

JASON. 'Intended wings.' How depressing.

MICHAEL. Yes. Makes them into suicides, really, the pigeons.

JASON. No – no, it doesn't. It could mean the wings were *intended* to carry them upwards, out of the darkness, but they were defective in some way, these wings, so the pigeons aren't suicidal, not at all, just badly equipped for flying. Like the rest of us.

MICHAEL. But still, the way he wrote it the wings are O.K. They extend. They extend but the pigeons sink – sink on extended – (*Gestures.*) is the point. 'Ambiguously undulating' is the point.

JASON *pours himself another glass, is aware of* MICHAEL *watching him.*

JASON. What's up?

MICHAEL. Nothing. Nothing's up. Why?

JASON. Oh, just – just – but you look as if something's up. Are you expecting old Neets, is that it?

MICHAEL. What?

JASON. Old Neets, are you expecting her?

MICHAEL. I wish you'd stop referring to her as old Neets. It makes her sound unhygienic.

JASON. I got it from you. That's what you call her.

MICHAEL. No, I don't. Not any more. I've made a point of calling her Anita.

JASON. So you have. As if it were two words. An Eeta. An Eeta. Like a measurement. Don't you move an eeta or I shoot –

MICHAEL. I'm on my ninth bloody draft, do you realise that? I've been around the track eight times with this novel, over two – what is it? – nearly two and a half years, and I'm not making it better, I'm just making more drafts. I feel completely untalented.

JASON. Well, you're not. At least three of the six or seven drafts I've read are good enough to be published. Not all three of them, I don't mean, but any one of them. With a bit of redrafting. (*Laughs.*) That one you sent to – that chap, that agent, Weeble –

MICHAEL. Weedon. His name is Weedon.

JASON. Weedon. Sorry. Anyway, Weedon wanted to take you on and he should know, shouldn't he? Why don't you trust him?

MICHAEL. Because at the moment I don't trust anybody, least of all myself. I don't even believe in the title any more.

JASON. 'Some Fitful Fevers', it's a good title.

MICHAEL. What?

JASON. 'Some Fitful Fevers'. It's O.K.

MICHAEL. That's not the title. That was never a title. It was just a way of identifying it, at the beginning. The very beginning. Instead of 'work in progress'.

JASON. Well, what's the title now?

MICHAEL. 'Antelopes in Antibes'.

There is a pause.

JASON. Why?

MICHAEL. It has a meaning.

JASON. It must be in the ninth draft. There weren't any antelopes in the ones I read. And nobody went to Antibes.

MICHAEL. Do you like her?

JASON. Who? Oh. An Eeta. Yes, I do. Yes, she seems very – very – from what I've seen. Why?

MICHAEL. Well, I think I need to know what you think of her. How you see her.

JASON. Oh. (*Takes out joint, begins to roll it.*) Well, as – um, a bit of a waif, I suppose.

MICHAEL. A waif? Well, yes – of course she is, with her background, those parents, she's bound to be a waif, isn't she, no choice – in fact, what's amazing about her, truly amazing, now that I come to think of it, is not that she's a waif, 'a bit of a waif' as you put it, but that she's a – a strong and individual sort of – sort of waif. Don't you think?

JASON *nods.*

MICHAEL. So – so you don't mind her staying here sometimes, spending the night?

JASON. Not at all. Well, sometimes a bit but never seriously.

MICHAEL. What times do you mind?

JASON. Well, when she – oh, the obvious things. You know.

MICHAEL. No, I don't know. What things?

JASON. It gets crowded in the kitchen when I'm hungover in the morning.

MICHAEL. Well then, that makes a lot of times. As you're hungover most mornings. God, I hate the smell of pot.

JASON. Neets – An-Eeta doesn't. She smokes it too. Haven't you noticed?

MICHAEL. Yes, well – I don't like the smell when she does it, either.

JASON. But you haven't said anything to her, have you?

MICHAEL. The point is she's not – she hasn't – well, she's still a guest. So of course I haven't said anything. But

I might. Soon. That's the point. But what worries me is – is that I've started worrying about her. I mean, when I should be working I start thinking, thinking, well, she ought to be bloody here by now, and where is she, and then a sort of worry grows, just a little one, never specific, not about her being run over or assaulted or – meeting somebody else, for God's sakes, least of all that – it's more – a worry over the mystery of her – of who she is. That's what worries me about her absence, her lateness – not where or what or why – but who. Who is she? Perhaps the point is – the real point is – that I'm in love with her. I've never felt like that about any of the others. Have you ever known me feel like that?

JASON. You used to get very excited about Ingrid.

MICHAEL. Ingrid! But that was just the sex. She was an addiction. A brief addiction.

JASON. And a bloody noisy one. You know, there's a funny echo that starts in your bedroom and ends up in mine. Seems to run around in the walls –

MICHAEL. You can hear us?

JASON. You and Ingrid, she used to honk, or by the time it went around in the walls it was a honk, like an angry goose.

MICHAEL. And what do you hear these days?

JASON. Not much. It's all right.

MICHAEL. She's very careful, when you're around. Gets embarrassed. But our sex is – as if – as if we both – reach out to some place where we're quite, quite – well, beyond ourselves – free and without inhibitions. You know, the last time we suddenly began to strip each other, just pulled each other's clothes –

JASON. Yeah, Mychy, I don't think you should, I really don't think you should – leave it to my imagination, and then leave it to me not to imagine it – I mean, with your 'oops-a-daisy' – one-two and oops-a-daisy –

MICHAEL. What? What did you say?

JASON. Well – you know, when you go oops-a-daisy, one-two and oops-a-daisy –

MICHAEL. Are you – are you suggesting it's obscene or something?

JASON. No, no, just a bit – a bit public, that's all. Bit difficult to look at when it's going on in front of one. One of her family's mating rituals, is it, passed on from generation to generation –

MICHAEL. It's a game. An affectionate expression of – of a kind of joie de vivre. I'm sorry if it offends you.

JASON. No, no, it doesn't offend me –

MICHAEL. Then why mention it?

JASON. Sorry – sorry, but as you were asking –

MICHAEL. I wasn't asking anything. I was explaining. Trying to explain my need to have her here, in here, living with me, officially. That's really what I'm trying to do. Take it into account, from your point of view.

JASON. You sure you don't want to get married and have done with it?

MICHAEL. No.

JASON. Well, that's all right then.

MICHAEL. What is?

JASON. That you're sure you don't want to get married.

MICHAEL. No, what I said is that I'm not sure I don't want to get married. I am, in fact, very far from not sure. But you clearly took me to mean the opposite. Which must mean that you're the one that's not sure I should marry her.

JASON. It was a misunderstanding – a rather complicated double negative that doesn't come out as a positive – muddled semantics, that's all, Mychy. 'Sure' is one of those words that – that –

MICHAEL. Christ, I'm trying to have one of the most serious conversations of my life, the most serious –

JASON. But I'm being serious. I'm doing the most serious listening of my life, Mychy. I'm being – being – Look. (*Stubs out joint, drains off glass, puts it away from him.*) You're in a state. You see.

MICHAEL. Yes, well. Sorry.

JASON. I'm only trying to say –

MICHAEL. Yeah, I know. It's just that – you always have such a casual attitude with your own – (*Gestures.*) things – with women. So I assume you're being rather casual with me. About mine.

JASON. I don't feel at all casual about yours. There's a lot at stake. For both of us.

MICHAEL. For both of us?

JASON. Well, all three of us, come to that. But for you and old – her.

MICHAEL. And for you, you're saying.

JASON. If you're married then it's all different. Obviously. Completely different from the present set-up.

MICHAEL. Is it really, when it comes down to it? After all, she's already got a key.

JASON. She's borrowed a key. No, I mean – you've lent her a key. But she only uses it when you – allow her to, really. She understands the implications – that's why she always rings the bell before she lets herself in.

MICHAEL. Still, you don't like her having it at all, do you?

JASON *says nothing.*

MICHAEL. You don't.

JASON. Well, actually I suppose I do find it a bit odd, awkward, actually when I come back sometimes and she's let herself in without either of us being here. (*Little pause.*) I mean, as you ask, Mychy.

MICHAEL. Odd, awkward – to be alone with my girlfriend?

JASON. Wrong words. Not odd, awkward – it's just, well, finding somebody else in the house, somebody I scarcely know coming and going, when I'm not expecting it. That's all. But now I'm beginning to expect it so I'm getting used to it, I really am. I mean, to hell with the bloody key, it's completely beside the point.

MICHAEL. But the point it's beside is you. You don't want me to marry her. You think I'm making a mistake. That's the truth, isn't it?

JASON. Look – aren't we rather forgetting old – Anita in all this? We're rather taking it for granted – I mean, have you discussed it with her?

MICHAEL. No. I've only just begun to discuss it with myself. Now I'm discussing it with you. Do you think she might refuse me, then? It hadn't occurred to me. Why should she? Do you think she would? (*Looks at watch.*) Now she's really late. Why should she? She loves me.

JASON. Oh, she's said so, has she?

MICHAEL. Yes, yes, she has – I think she has, I'm sure she has, anyway she behaves as if she has.

JASON. And you, what have you said?

MICHAEL. I haven't had to say anything. She knows. She's very instinctual.

JASON. Yes.

MICHAEL. What does that mean?

JASON. Well, nothing, it means yes. You tell me she's very instinctual and I say yes – Jesus, Mychy!

MICHAEL. Have you heard something?

JASON. Like what?

MICHAEL. About her instincts – instinctuality?

JASON. No, of course not. (*Laughs.*) Who would I hear it from – except you. Things you've reported. That she's said to you.

MICHAEL. What sort of things?

JASON (*rolling another joint*). That you're not the first and only. There have been others before you.

MICHAEL (*sarcastically*). Before me, yes, well, she wouldn't be telling me about the ones she's having at the same time. Or after me. Yet. I trust.

JASON *lets out a strange eruption of laughter.*

MICHAEL. What?

JASON. Jesus, Mychy, I keep telling you I don't know anything about her really except what you tell me. I've scarcely even had a conversation with her.

MICHAEL. Well, hardly surprising as from your own account you're either hungover or irritated by her turning up. Perhaps if you tried talking to her some time, made a bit of an effort – you know, for my sake.

JASON. Yes, yes, I will, I will – but what we're talking about at the moment, what we're discussing at the moment is – is not me and her but you and her – and your sexual jealousy, isn't that it?

MICHAEL. My what? Don't be – don't be so bloody – sexual jealousy!

JASON. Ah. So it's not that that's made you worried and blocked and suddenly desperate to get married.

MICHAEL. Desperate? Desperate! I'm not at all desperate! Just considering.

JASON. Just considering – oh well, that's O.K. then. That's fine.

MICHAEL. But what is quite clear, absolutely clear, is that you're against my marrying her, aren't you?

JASON. No, no, of course I'm not – but – well, what about the house?

MICHAEL. The house?

JASON. Yes. Our house. If you set up together, I mean really set up together – permanently – whether married or not – well, I'd have to move out, wouldn't I?

MICHAEL. Would you?

JASON. Well, yes, obviously.

MICHAEL. But this is a – is a – you're virtually making me choose. It's like some Spanish, Spanish – mediaeval Spanish poem, epic poem – it's a kind of blackmail. I mean, where would you go, I'd feel guilty. Treacherous.

JASON. Why should you, it would be my decision and – and perhaps I need to get away anyway – and there's that job, I've been thinking about it a lot, it's probably still open.

MICHAEL. Job, what job?

JASON. The British Council job. In New Guinea.

MICHAEL. What? Oh, that job! It isn't even in New Guinea. It's in Guyana.

JASON. Yes, Guyana, the West Indies. One of the islands. And they play cricket. Test matches, now I come to think of it.

MICHAEL. No, they don't. It's the place it always rains, so they're always cancelled, and it's not even an island, it's a tip of somewhere South American and it's hot, steamy, jungly.

JASON. Are you sure? Still, it's a place to start, it's a university job, that's what matters, and who knows, I might end up as a professor, Professor Cartts of the South American jungle.

MICHAEL. No, you wouldn't, with your – your (*Gestures.*) health, you'd end up as plain Mr Cartts – Mr Cartts he dead. And you know it. And that's what I mean by blackmail. Because you know I'd never let you – never –

JASON. And how the fuck – how the fuck – do you think you can stop me? (*Little pause.*) I'm going to go, whether you marry – marry An-eeta or not.

MICHAEL. Then I'm fucking well not going to marry her, whether you go or not! So you can fuck off anywhere you want to, Japes, just as long as you fuck off! (*Going off.*)

JASON. I thought people like us weren't supposed to end arguments with language – language –

Sound of MICHAEL *going upstairs.*

JASON (*gets up. He has a crippled leg. Limps to door, bellowing*) – of such fucking – fucking – ! (*Stops, limps back, forces himself to settle down with joint. Takes a swig of wine.*) 'Complacencies of the peignoir, and late / Coffee and oranges in a sunny chair' –

Sound of MICHAEL *starting up furious typing, above.*

JASON *looks up, makes a gesture of derision, concentrates.*

JASON.
'And the green freedom of a cockatoo
Upon a rug mingle to dissipate
The holy hush of ancient sacrifice
She dreams a little – '

ANITA *enters during the above.*

JASON. You didn't ring the bell so it can't be you, can it?

ANITA. Well, it is. (*Looking up towards sound of typing.*)

JASON. Yes, that's him all right. He's in a state. All because of you. You're late, you see. Where have you been?

ANITA. Oh, at that church. St Mark's. I wanted to do a bit of drawing and I love it there, I really love it.

JASON. Oh yes, St Mark's, Mummy was very, very fond of it, you know, she was a friend, an official friend of St Mark's, sat on committees, helped to raise money, probably wanted to be buried there. Daddy too of course – just in time apparently, it's getting quite crowded.

ANITA. He wasn't really, was he? In a state? Because of me, my being late? I mean mostly he never notices whether I'm there or not.

JASON. Well, you see, he's only just noticed that he's in love with you.

ANITA. There, I knew it. I told you so.

JASON. Well, you were right, weren't you? That's why you're in trouble. Being in love with you is blocking his writing. Stops for minutes on end. To pester me about you. Then he's back up there and off again. And it's all – all circular. Like a lavatory roll that never unrolls to the end, just keeps renewing itself. Probably just as well as it's crap, really. Just crap.

ANITA. Crap? Is it really?

JASON. Delicately thought, finely wrought, maturely paced, ironically poised crap. Well, you've read some of it.

ANITA. Yes, but I wouldn't know, it's all above my head, isn't it – but – but poor Mychy – (*Looking up.*)

JASON (*also looking up*). Terrifying, isn't it? And moving too, in its way. But the thing is, Neets, it doesn't matter. Not really. Because he'll be a success, you'll see. He inherited the success gene from Daddy. And just as Daddy put up blocks of flats that everybody bought and nobody wanted to live in, old Mychy will put out novels that everybody will buy and nobody will read. So don't you worry about it, Anita. He's going to be O.K., old Mychy.

ANITA. And what gene did you inherit, Japes?

JASON. I think – I think Mummy's driving gene. Yes.

ANITA. Shut up, Japes, that's not funny.

JASON. I wasn't trying to be funny. Mummy was a very good driver. Ace. Only had the one fatal accident. And I've never believed she was driving – I think Daddy was. But perhaps they both were. They always liked to do everything together. I must show you their grave some time, up at St Mark's.

ANITA. But what does he mean, he's in love with me? Or is he just saying things?

JASON. No, no, he means – he means – well, the fact is, Neets, (*Little pause.*) he wants to marry you. I think he's going to, you know, pop – pop it at you. The question.

ANITA. Oh, Christ! Well, can't you tell him?

JASON (*after a pause*). Tell him what?

ANITA. Well – that there's nothing to me really – not the sort of things he needs – the darks and the depths and the troubled turmoils and all that sort of stuff.

JASON. You've got a gift.

ANITA. Gift? What gift – he can't mean my drawing – he doesn't think I'm some sort of artist?

JASON. No, no, of course he doesn't.

ANITA. What, then?

JASON. Well, just sort of, you know, being. Being Neets. Old Neets. Very, very desirable old Neets.

ANITA. Ah, you mean he loves me for myself alone!

JASON. Well, (*Little pause.*) and the sex, of course. I stopped the details.

ANITA (*after a little pause*). Yes, well. I should bloody hope so.

JASON. The question I ask – very seriously, Neets – is – what do you want from him? Eh? What do you want from my big brother?

ANITA (*after a pause*). You know what I want. I want the little brother, you see, Japes.

JASON. But you already have the little brother. Sometimes on the same day as you have the big one.

ANITA. Don't! Don't! Don't you do that!

JASON. Sorry. I'm sorry, Neets. Anyway, we're going to stop it. You're just going to be my little – my little sister, possibly even sister-in-law – isn't that the way it's got to work?

ANITA. It won't work for me. I've been thinking about it, Japes, I've never thought about anything so hard – and this is the thing, the difference – when I'm with you and I think about him, that I'm being unfaithful to him – well, even then I'm not ashamed about him. But when I'm with him and I think about you, that I'm being unfaithful to you, then I feel – I feel quite disgusting, Japes. You see.

JASON. Well, once you stop thinking about me when you're with him, you'll feel O.K. Perfectly O.K.

ANITA. But don't you at least get jealous?

JASON. Yes. But I don't like it. After all, it's only sex. Nothing to get jealous about, really, these days, when there's so much of it around. (*Laughs.*) The only thing I mind, really mind – (*Imitating her.*) one – two – and oops-a-daisy, one – two and oops-a-daisy, now that's disgusting, you're both disgusting when you do that. Pass me my stuff.

ANITA *passes his joint stuff, pours herself a glass of wine.*

JASON *starts on joint, passes it to* ANITA, *who passes him glass of wine. They interchange thus during the following.*

ANITA. So what you're saying is, marry him, as far as you're concerned. Right, Japes?

JASON. No, I'm not. I'm bloody not. What I'm saying is – do what you want – but do it with your whole self. Existentially, see.

ANITA. I don't want to marry him.

JASON. Good. Because you shouldn't. Nor should he. He shouldn't marry you. So stop fretting and enjoy your fucking.

ANITA. And what about you?

JASON. I'm going to sort myself out, it's time – (*Nods.*) might even go away, far away to the tropics, set myself up as a university prof. Write my own novel. And it won't be draft after draft, it'll be like Mummy's driving – zoom! I'll zoom over the finishing line. Believe me?

ANITA (*shakes her head, kisses him*). You're bloody useless, that's what you are, Japes.

JASON. I've had my uses, though, haven't I? (*Strokes her breast.*)

ANITA (*shudders*). Ooh, don't, don't, Japes.

JASON. You're such a – such a kitten, you are. That's why we love you really. Because we love kittens. And you're the only one we've got. Purr. Go on. Purr for me.

ANITA *makes slight purring noises, rubbing her breast against his hand.*

They begin to make frantic love. Typing above stops. They continue. Sound of footsteps upstairs. They become suddenly aware.

ANITA *leaps up, dashes out. Sound of* MICHAEL *coming downstairs.* JASON *trying to assume dopey position. Sound of* ANITA *closing front door as:*

MICHAEL *enters.*

MICHAEL. Hi.

JASON. Oh, hi. (*Stirring himself.*) You look – what do you look? Transformed. Fulfilled.

MICHAEL. Yes, well, suddenly – floodgates – floodgates again – sorry about all that stuff – (*Little laugh.*) – don't know what got into me – but Christ, (*Sniffing.*) you've been going at it, Japes – actually I had some idea she was here, seemed to hear the bell at some point.

JASON. No. Absolutely no bell. I'd have heard it.

There is a ring at the door.

JASON. How's that for timing?

MICHAEL *goes towards door as sound of door, off, opening.*

MICHAEL (*off*). Hi, Anita, hi, hi, hi!

ANITA. Hi.

Little pause, then off.

MICHAEL *and* ANITA. One – two – and oops-a-daisy! One – two – and oops-a –

JASON *flinches.*

Lights.

Scene Two

Five years later.

ANITA *is lying rumpled on the sofa.* JASON *is straightening out his clothes. There are pages of a student's essay scattered about.*

ANITA. Are you all right?

JASON. Yes, yes, thanks, Neets. A bit jet-lagged still, I expect. (*Looks at her.*) Sorry.

ANITA. That's all right. It was great to have you back where you belong.

JASON. Mmm? (*Picking up pages.*)

ANITA. We always say. You always say.

JASON. Are there some over there? Some of these?

ANITA *picks up pages from sofa, hands them to him.*

JASON. Thanks.

ANITA. It isn't then?

JASON. What?

ANITA. Great to be back – it's been nearly a year this time. Actually yes, a year.

JASON. I know. A difficult year. A long and difficult year.

ANITA. Because you've missed being here? (*Has been straightening herself out, feeling about beneath her uncomfortably.*)

JASON. Well, that too, of course. But everything. The faculty politics, island politics –

ANITA. All that stuff you were telling Mychy about last night?

JASON. Yes, that stuff.

ANITA (*fishing out page from under her bottom*). There's this.

JASON. Oh. Thanks. There's still a page missing –

ANITA. Oh. Well, it's not here. (*Looking around sofa.*) It's very precious then? I mean you seem very worried about it.

JASON. Well, it's a student's essay. One of my best students. That's why I wanted to show it to you. As I'd been talking about it. I thought you – you were showing an interest.

ANITA. Yes, well – I thought you were trying to tell me something.

JASON. What sort of something?

ANITA. Well, not about Wordsworth. I've never even read Wordsworth, to my knowledge.

JASON. Well, what else, what sort of something else – ?

ANITA. About her.

JASON. Her? Oh, her. Sajit. Yes, well, I suppose I was – because you were asking, you and Mychy keep asking why I go on doing it, teaching English in Guyana in what Mychy calls the educational arsehole of the world –

ANITA. I've never heard him call it that.

JASON. Well, that's how he thinks of it, I know he does – and you obviously can't see the point either –

ANITA. Well, for different reasons, probably. Or no, perhaps the same reason – well, we both wish you were back here, don't we, obviously? That's all.

JASON. Yes, well, I sort of hoped Sajit would explain – this would explain – why I go on doing it, that's all. I mean, look, she's bright, and quick and has a feeling for language, our language –

ANITA *has begun to roll a joint.*

JASON. – and the only literature she's got is our literature, an accidental literature, here's all this poetry, Wordsworth's – I mean, just think of it – even if you haven't read him you'd know his – his countryside, his world –

Three years she grew in sun and shower;
Then Nature said, 'A lovelier flower
On earth was never sown;
This child I to myself will take;
She shall be mine, and I will make
A lady of my own.

Myself will to my darling be
Both law and impulse: and with me
The girl, in rock and plain –
In earth and heaven, in glade and bower.
Shall feel an overseeing power
To kindle and restrain.
She shall be sportive as the fawn – (*Stops.*)

– but Sajit, however hard she tries to imagine it, any of it – glades, bowers, fawns, sportive fawns – they're not in her blood, she probably has to look them up in a dictionary. But I can help, you see, that's the point for me. I can help her to imagine.

ANITA. Are you in love with her?

JASON. What! Oh, Neets! She's a student.

ANITA. Oh, Japes! (*Imitating him.*) So was I, remember?

JASON. Yes, well – you weren't my student.

ANITA. Wasn't I? Sometimes I feel as if I was. But left half-done. Anyway – anyway, Japes, you're different. Not the way you're usually different when you come back – and it's not just not boozing. It's as if something happened. I mean – are you in love with somebody, well, you're bound to be some day, but I think I've a right to know, honestly, Japes, don't you?

JASON. You'll be the first to know, Neets. I'm not not drinking and doping because of some – some girl – honestly! (*Laughs.*) It was just that it was getting so bad, that's all.

ANITA. Well, something's happened – something's happened this last year, I know it has.

JASON. No, nothing, Neets. Nothing's *happened* to do with – to do with – falling in love, anyway. Though actually something did happen to get me off the booze at last. I don't know if I should tell you this. (*Little pause.*) Well, there was this friend, you see, an American. We did some seminars together and – well, in the evenings, virtually every evening actually, we went down to a rum shop – Angry Annie's – and we got into fights. Well, he did. He's that sort of American. Very political. Thinks anybody who isn't fighting for black independence is a fascist or a coward, that sort of thing – and he liked to stir it up at Annie's, you know, pick out the largest black guy in the room, and go over and sort of cuddle him and – and insult him at the same time – tell him he ought to be out there hanging whitey from the lamp posts, not hanging about with types like him, 'Look at me, the colour of my skin, what's the matter with you, you a faggot, a big black cowardly fascist faggot?' – that sort of thing, and mostly they'd just push him away and he'd pass out – me too, sometimes – pass out – but sometimes they'd beat him up. Which is what he really wanted, I suppose. Anyway – anyway, one night he picked out this really tough, really tough – who just beat him and beat him until he was down on his knees, his head hanging, vomiting and blood – and I – I don't know why, I still don't understand it but anyway I – I – joined in. I – I beat him, beat him and beat him. Harry, I mean. My friend. Not the black – in fact the black had to drag me off him. Off Harry. So – so – Harry went to hospital. I visited him a couple of times. He had no idea – but he was gone really – here (*Touches his head.*) – the Dean sent him home – and I – don't do it any more. Any of it. I stay in my bungalow and I mark my essays and prepare my classes and – get on with my novel. Try to keep myself intact, you see. To be intact and finish my novel. You see?

ANITA (*after a pause*). Mychy says it's very good. When are you going to let me read it?

JASON. Oh well, if you really want to –

ANITA (*angrily*). Of course I want to.

JASON. Well, he's bringing it back from that agent of his – Weedon – this afternoon. So if Weedon thinks it's O.K. I'll have the confidence – (*Gestures.*)

ANITA. Huh! (*Little laugh.*) A whole year – you've no idea, Japes, how you've conditioned me somehow, so there's not a day when you're not here, when you're not here, (*Holds her breasts.*) not a day when I don't go into your room and lie on your bed and – and pray that when you are here, soon, please soon, you'll still want me – were you ever in love with me? Ever?

JASON. I've never been in love with anybody else. Never expect to be.

ANITA (*after a little pause*). Hah! First you give up dope, then you give up booze, now you give up me, then you'll be in love at last. That's the way it'll go. It must.

JASON. But the thing is, Neets –

ANITA. Go on. Say it.

JASON. You know.

ANITA. Still, I want you to say it.

JASON. Well, we can't. Ever again. I meant us not to.

ANITA. But you couldn't resist me, was that it? Or was it out of kindness? Poor little Neets – old Neets – expecting her – expecting her – why did you come back at all then, why don't you just keep away, getting yourself more and more intact until you're dead to me. That would be the kindness.

JASON. But I need to see – to see –

ANITA. Who? Mychy? Or your daughter? Which?

JASON (*little pause*). All of you. You're my family. All I have for a family, Neets. And I love you. All of you. And that's why – that's really why –

ANITA. Japes, don't be disgusting. Honest is what you used to be. With your whole heart. Existential.

JASON. I am being honest. I need you all.

ANITA. Well, I don't see why I should need you any more. I think I should try not to do that. And your daughter doesn't need you, does she, she only knows you in bits of time as it is, so you have no idea of what she goes through in her life, of what Mychy and I go through – you know, Japes, you've betrayed me, you said you couldn't, you were too feeble and frail, you couldn't cope – but look at you, look at you, Jason, standing there perfectly *intact* – wishing if only you hadn't had your usual coming home fuck – you could have taken the two of us with you, you should have – should have –

JASON. But how could I have, we don't even know if she's mine.

ANITA. I know. I know whose she is. And so do you.

JASON. No, I don't. And nor do you. Medically speaking, it's quite impossible for either of us to know.

ANITA. She's yours, Wendy's yours, she's yours. Do you know how hard it is for me with him? (*Long pause.*) Do you know how hard?

JASON. But you love him. You said you loved him.

ANITA. I said what you both wanted to hear.

JASON. Then you shouldn't have.

ANITA *runs at him, slapping at him.*

ANITA. Get out, get out, get out of my house. Get out of my home, get out. Get out!

JASON *lurches backwards.*

Sound of front door opening, closing.

MICHAEL (*off*). Hi. Hi.

Sound of front door closing.

JASON *seizes stick, scrambles desperately out of room, as:*

ANITA *scrambles to sofa, sits down.*

ANITA. Hi, darling. (*Picks joint out of ashtray.*)

MICHAEL (*off, clearly taking off coat, etc.*). It's turned bloody cold, no heating in the taxi – (*Enters, carrying a briefcase.*) Hi, darling. (*Beams at* ANITA.) Hi.

ANITA. Hi. Well, you're looking very full of yourself, where have you been?

MICHAEL. Well, with Weedon. Talking about Japes's novel. He thinks it's full of talent. Brimming with talent. A real original. Desperate to take him on.

ANITA. Well, you said he'd like it, didn't you. Clever old Japes. And how's Weedon, darling? How are his cats? How's his parrot?

MICHAEL. Cockatoo, (*Raising an admonishing finger.*) we have to remember that it's a cockatoo, not a parrot, and that it's name is Dolly, not Polly, and they're all fine and he's fine, at least in some senses of the word, no, no, in no sense of the word is Weedon *fine*, ever, he must have put on half a stone in the last few weeks, in fact he's almost obese – (*Picking up ashtray, taking it to wastepaper basket.*)

ANITA. What are you doing?

MICHAEL. Emptying the ashtray.

ANITA. But I haven't finished it.

MICHAEL. Oh. (*Looks into ashtray, brings it back, takes out joint, gives it to her.*) Sorry, darling, I wasn't trying to make a point, how could I, when I give interviews about the permissibility of the permissive society – it's just the smell, seems to get into my sinuses these days –

ANITA. Oh, well, I don't really want it anyway. (*Dropping it into ashtray.*)

MICHAEL. No, no, honestly, darling –

ANITA. Please dump it! (*Checking irritation.*) I've got to pick up Wendy in a minute, so I shouldn't.

MICHAEL. Oh, then we'll put it over here, you can finish it when you get back.

ANITA. Thank you.

There is a pause. MICHAEL *looks at her.*

MICHAEL. Darling, you all right?

ANITA. Yes, fine, fine. Where did he take you, Weedon? Oh, to L'Epicure, I suppose, as usual.

MICHAEL. The Garrick Club. He's been threatening me with it for months, and I've kept stalling him, don't know why, never liked the idea of it, I suppose, a club full of actors, lawyers, judges, agents – actually I've never liked the idea of a club full of anyone, really, as I'm completely unclubable, aren't I? You know, I always think of it as Daddy's sort of thing, he was actually on the committee of the Garrick at one time, we used to hate the way he'd say it with this face, with a shy – a shy sort of smirk on his face, Japes does a terrific imitation – so. He sort of swindled me into it. Got me into a taxi, just as he always does when he's taking me to L'Epicure, and I didn't notice he'd taken me to the Garrick instead until we were actually there. I pointed out that I couldn't go in, as I was improperly dressed – (*Pats his throat.*) so he took one out of his pocket, looped it around my neck and knotted it – all very fluent, as if he'd practised, the bugger. Perhaps it's some rite of passage – when your latest has nestled in among the best sellers for three months running, which IN PERVERTED COMMAS has, he informed me over his third and my only brandy. He insisted I keep it. As a memento. (*Takes tie out of pocket, hands it to* ANITA.)

ANITA (*attempting to snap to attention, studies it*). God, darling it's ghastly – where did you get it?

MICHAEL. From Weedon, darling, I've just told you.

ANITA. Sorry, sorry, Mychy – I was trying to follow, but sometimes you're too quick – you know how dim I am, especially when you've been drinking –

MICHAEL. I haven't been drinking.

ANITA. I thought you said you'd put away three or four brandies.

MICHAEL. One brandy. One brandy, I said. Which I nursed. A glass and a half – if that, of claret.

ANITA. Well, that's a lot for you. That's drinking. I didn't say you were drunk. Only that you'd been drinking and I couldn't follow you and – and I've only had that, that bit of a joint and – and – (*Breaks down.*)

MICHAEL. Darling, what is it? What's the matter? What's happened?

ANITA. Nothing, nothing's happened, it's just – Wendy, worrying about Wendy, I've been worrying and worrying about her. All day. Every minute of the day.

MICHAEL. Has there been more trouble, then? Something at school?

ANITA. No, no, it's just her! Well, you know yourself, Mychy, perfectly well, she doesn't get on with people, her own peer group, or with us – she's always miserable and sullen and ill-tempered, Michael, she is, and tantrums the moment she doesn't get her own way – nobody likes her, nobody likes our Wendy, Mychy, nobody.

MICHAEL. Now that isn't strictly true, darling, look at – look at – Japes. Absolutely fallen in love with her, when he put her to bed the other night he had her yelping with laughter with his 'Here comes the bogeyman', and he actually got her to sing, all quite gooey really, but there's a real bond there – it's not just that he's brought something out in her, she's brought something out in him.

ANITA. Yes, well, he only does it a couple of times a year, when he bothers to come back, let him try doing it every night, then we'd see how gooey – gooey –

MICHAEL. Well, she's not really Japes's responsibility, in that sense, is she, I only mentioned him because you said that nobody – and anyway she's only four, for God's sake, she's not a hardened war criminal, just a – a perfectly normal, normal difficult child, you know the real problem, the real problem is that we're not allowed to accept old-fashioned normal difficult children – nowadays every infant has to conform to some rule of growth – a touch of colic, a few teething problems, some mandatory hiccoughs in the toilet training. Well, it didn't work like that in our daughter's case, did it, every aspect of her growth so far – from getting her wires crossed at the nappy stage to gum-boils and thrush and – but then she didn't just – just pop out of you, did she, in spite of all those natural birth classes we had to sit through – she didn't get classes in the womb, there she was, perfectly innocently upside down or the wrong way around and suddenly she was being jerked out by forceps and clamps – put any creature, especially a new one, in a bad temper, so that's all it comes from really, this famous bad temper of hers, her beginnings, and all we have to do, darling, really, is to be patient until she recovers it. Her temper. Or discovers it. And then her behaviour will be – well, merely as bad as everybody else's. (*Little pause.*) And in the meanwhile we can look at some other nursery schools if you want.

ANITA. No, Mychy, no, the truth is – we should keep her at home. Yes. That's the proper thing, you know it is.

MICHAEL. At home! But darling, I work here – and you – now you've really started on your children's book again – the bedbugs, Basil the Bashful –

ANITA. Boris. It's Boris.

MICHAEL. Boris. I couldn't bear it if you had to give up on him again.

ANITA. We could get an au pair.

MICHAEL. An au pair! But we haven't got room for an au pair! Where would we put her?

ANITA. In Japes's room. Well, it's just sitting there wasted for most of the year –

MICHAEL. But darling, it's his. His room. Whether he's in it or not. He still keeps a good part of his life in it.

ANITA. We could shift all that down to the basement. And when he does decide to turn up, he can doss down in here.

MICHAEL. In here. (*Looks around.*) Japes. Doss down in – (*Laughs.*) legally half of every room in the house belongs to him, have you forgotten?

ANITA. We could buy him out.

MICHAEL. No, I couldn't. He'd never sell. And I wouldn't want to buy – buy him! – he was born here. I was here when he was born here. It'll always be here for him, wherever he is.

ANITA. Just like you, you mean?

MICHAEL. What?

ANITA. You'll always be here for him, wherever he is, which is why he hasn't gone anywhere, really, not even to Guyana, not in his – his soul. He's even trying to turn himself into you, not just – just cleaning himself up but becoming a writer and – and even trying to muscle in on Weedon, he's busy sort of – sort of taking over from you, being you –

MICHAEL. What!

ANITA. Yes. You but without any of the responsibilities of – of a proper grown-up. And you let – no, you encourage him, the heart of him, the soul of him, because he's your little brother and you can't bear to see him get free of you. Your little Japes. Belongs to you. Big Mychy and his little Japes. Well, I want him out, I want that room for my daughter. My daughter's au pair.

MICHAEL. I thought – I thought you loved him.

ANITA. Love him, love him, what's that got to do with it, it's not my love that won't let him move out, it's yours, and all the guilt, the guilt shit you mix up in it, the way you go on blaming yourself is a kind of conceit, anything that happens to him good or bad, it always goes back to you and what you did to him, so really you end up as a sort of God and he's just your playmate. Thing. Plaything.

MICHAEL. This isn't you, this isn't Neets, my Neets. It isn't, Neets. It isn't you.

ANITA. You didn't cripple him on purpose, you were just boys, horsing about in a swimming pool, bouncing each other on a diving board, nothing glamorous or dark or hidden in it, just a simple bloody accident, however you tell it after we fuck, your voice droning on and on with the damage you've done to him, oh woe is me, woe is me that I could mangle mine own brother, while all the time your daughter, who's in need, real need of your love and care and attention, is denied – denied – (*Turns away.*)

MICHAEL. What? Oh, Neets – my dearest old Neets – (*Goes to her.*) please, my darling, you can't believe, mustn't believe, ever, that I've made some choice between – between Japes and our Wendy – or you and – and – I love you all. To the very best of my – my – I do. And he is breaking free, you know, Japes – his whole thing over there in Guyana, his struggle to become healthy and strong, his taking his job seriously, his writing – that's all part of his trying to make a new life for himself. With the woman he loves.

ANITA. Loves? Woman he loves?

MICHAEL. One of his students, inevitably. She's called Rabbit, no, of course she isn't, Sab – Rab something like that. Anyway the point is that he absolutely adores her, they're head over heels, the two of them.

JASON *enters.*

MICHAEL *breaks away.*

JASON. Ah, you're back then, I thought I heard your voice.

MICHAEL. Yes, I was just coming to look for you, things to tell you, but I was just filling Neets in on the Garrick Club, remember Daddy in his Garrick Club days, that's where he took me, Weedon.

ANITA. Yes, do your face.

JASON. My face.

MICHAEL. That face you used to do that Daddy used to do whenever he was going off to the committee –

JASON. Oh. Oh, yes, that one – 'Oh, Debs darling, boys, quite forgotten that bloody Garrick pow-wow – '

MICHAEL (*laughs, looks towards* ANITA). Pow-wow, I'd forgotten pow-wow – only time he ever used the word – anyway, I was just telling Neets, Weedon made me wear a tie he'd brought along especially, wants to put me up for it, he thinks it's a good career move, I suppose, there are editors, possibly even a few literary editors, but just the thought of Daddy, and your smirking his smirk – better off, creatively anyway, on the outside, looking in.

JASON. Oh, but you're already on the inside, Mychy, at least as most of the reviewers see it.

MICHAEL. Well then, on the inside looking in. (*Laughs.*) Oh, and look – the fact is, I've been rather indiscreet with Neets, given the game away. About you and the lady in Guyana. Your Samji – it is Samji, isn't it, Japes, her name?

JASON. No, Sajit. It's Sajit.

ANITA. Sajit.

MICHAEL. Anyway, I just found myself blabbing it out, sorry, Japes.

ANITA. It would have been nicer to have heard from your own lips, Japes.

JASON. Yes, but well actually, it's not really that – that big a – at the moment it's still a friendship, really. Platonic.

MICHAEL. Platonic! It didn't sound at all platonic from your descriptions – steamy and jungly was the impression you gave me, one sexy lady. Not that she isn't brilliant with it, of course, she's got a real intelligence, Neets, marvellously simple and individual – have you shown Neets her essay?

JASON. No.

MICHAEL. You must read it, darling!

ANITA. Yes, well first there's a little matter of our daughter, our daughter, darling.

MICHAEL. What?

ANITA. It's time for me to collect her, I must dash or I'll be late again.

MICHAEL. Oh God, yes – (*Looking at his watch.*) See. Everything's all right. Everything's going to be fine. (*Puts his arms around her.*) In fact it's all going to be – one, two, one two and oops-a-daisy, one-two – (*Hoisting her up.*)

ANITA (*her legs clamped around him*). And oops-a-daisy, one-two and oops-a-daisy –

MICHAEL. What's this – you've got something – (*Hands go under skirt.*) here, got it! (*As* ANITA *unwraps herself* MICHAEL *is holding sheet of essay.*) What is it? (*Glances down at sheet.*)

ANITA (*looks at sheet, looks at* JASON). I've got to dash!

MICHAEL. Oh, darling – take a coat. It's turned cold again.

ANITA. Right. (*Goes out without coat.*)

MICHAEL (*bellowing*). Neets, a coat!

Sound of door shutting.

MICHAEL (*looks at essay*). I seem to recognise the handwriting. It's your lady's, isn't it? Her essay on Wordsworth. The Lucy poems. Yes, here's the quote. (*Glances down at sheet.*) 'Strange fits of passion have I known / And I will dare to tell / But in the lover's ear alone / What once to me befell' –

JASON. He really is tops, isn't he, old Bill. Old Billy Wordsworth.

MICHAEL (*nods, continues reciting, not reading*). 'When she I loved / Looked every day / As fresh as a flower in June / And I to her cottage made my way' –

JASON. Bent. Bent my way.

MICHAEL. Yes, of course. Bent my way.

JASON. 'Beneath the lowering moon' –

MICHAEL. 'Beneath the lowering moon'. (*Looks at* JASON.)

JASON. Well, thank God it turned up before I missed it, I get extremely neurotic about losing students' essays – it must have slipped onto the sofa while I was showing it to Neets. (*Holding out his hand for essay.*)

MICHAEL. But you haven't shown it to Neets yet, you said, didn't you say? Or she say? Or both say?

JASON. Ah, well when I was showing it to you, then.

MICHAEL. Ah, yes. Except it was in my study – you showed it to me in my study, didn't you. Well, anyway, better not tell your Samji that she ended up on the bum of your sister-in-law, however she got there, or she'll think – God knows what she'll think, eh? (*Handing him essay back.*)

JASON. Probably that we stint on the lavatory paper – eh? (*Lets out a kind of laugh.*)

MICHAEL (*smiles*). Well.

JASON. Well. (*Sees his manuscript.*) Well, how did it go?

MICHAEL. Mmmm?

JASON. With Weedon. My novel.

MICHAEL. Oh. Oh, yes. Torching the Dove. (*Picking the manuscript up.*) Not too well, actually, I'm afraid, Japes. He doesn't want to take you on, you see.

JASON. Ah. Thinks it stinks, does he?

MICHAEL. Not stinks, Japes, nothing you do could ever stink, for God's sake. No, he thinks you've got a talent, write beautifully, lots of good jokes about bad sex – 'lovely squalid stuff' were his words. And he admired – oh, lots of things. Everything except, well, except your tone, really.

JASON. My tone.

MICHAEL. Apparently it's identical to mine. My tone.

JASON. Your tone. And you, what do you think?

MICHAEL. Well, impossible for me to say, really, isn't it? I mean, if it is my tone, then I'd be too familiar with it – I'd be the last to know, so to speak, wouldn't I?

JASON. I can't imagine any tone less like yours than mine.

MICHAEL. Exactly. And I can't imagine any tone less like mine than yours. So it obviously cuts both ways. Our over-familiarity. Of course it's not a matter of imitation, the tone, but genetic – neither of us can help having that particular – tone gene. He thinks a lot of publishers would probably feel the same, that one of me is more than enough. Bloody awful being the younger brother sometimes, eh, Japes? Always the second comer, the second served. Neets was just saying as much a moment ago.

JASON. Oh, she was was she? Mychy, I think I'll go tomorrow.

MICHAEL. Oh. Not because of Weedon, I hope.

JASON. No, not because of Weedon. It's just that I rather find myself missing the educational arsehole. And the jungly smells.

MICHAEL. Well then – oddly enough, Neets was just saying that we should start thinking of an au pair, except there wasn't a room. (*Laughs.*)

JASON. Well, there is now. If you could see to packing up my things and shipping them – the bungalow needs them.

MICHAEL. And Samji does too, I expect. If she's to make a home with you.

JASON. It's Sajit, Mychy. Sajit. And I never let her anywhere near the bungalow. To tell you the truth, Mychy, she's just another of my fucks really.

MICHAEL. Really?

JASON. I've been in the habit of saving myself, my best self, for when I came home. You see.

MICHAEL. Ah. Well then. Perhaps under the circumstances you'd like to sell out. Your half of the house, that is.

JASON. Oh, I'd never want to do that. Too many important things have happened here. It means far too much to me to let go of it. Ever. (*Turns, goes out of the room.*)

Lights.

Scene Three

Seven years later.

Lights up on MICHAEL *on telephone.*

MICHAEL (*on telephone*). – oh, of course, sorry, fancy dress, I'd forgotten, they're all in fancy dress – well, she's there as a wolf – no, no, it's a fox, no, a wolf, I think – she's either there as a fox or a wolf, a girl too tall for her age with freckles as a fox or a wolf – and come to think of it, she may be in one of the corners lying down – is any of the girls there prostrate anywhere, on the floor? Pass me over to whom? Oh, Miss Stokehurst, (*Attempting calm.*) you're one of the teachers, are you, good – well, Miss Stokehurst, the point is we've lost Wendy – or rather you've lost Wendy – anyway, she's vanished from the party, the point is, you see – what? No, let me explain, let me explain – my wife is there somewhere with Mrs – your assistant headmistress – touring the building looking for – you see, the point is she 'phoned us, Wendy did, about half an hour ago, 'phoned us at home to say she wasn't feeling well, that she – she, well, as far as we could make out, some girl, some imbecile of a girl had given her pills – (*Little pause.*) yes, pills, red pills, that she'd somehow got hold of from her mother, presumably from her mother's bathroom or medicine cabinet or – or – anyway, she gave some to Wendy who swallowed them – yes, yes, that's right, that's the whole point, that's what I'm trying to tell you – she swallowed these bloody pills and then when she began to feel faint she 'phoned us and told us what she'd done and I told her to wait there, there and by the telephone, to try not to sit down or close her eyes, but when we got there she wasn't there so I've come back here in case she'd come here but my wife stayed there in case she was still there and she doesn't appear to be either here or there – so she – I suppose she set off from the school on her own – at this hour and dressed like a fox or a wolf and – yes, I know, very cold, very cold, and if she's coming across the heath – I mean, my God, across the heath in the dark in the cold, feeling faint and dressed like a wolf or a – the police, yes, perhaps we'd better – you'd better – look, Mrs – Mrs – where are you, where have you gone, where the hell have you gone? (*Shouting.*) Oh, darling, it's you, where have you been, where the hell have you been, she's not here, Wendy isn't here – what? A joke! Not pills, well, what the hell were they? What, smarties! Well – well, that's all right then and – and there you are, the two of you and – well, the thing is, darling, to calm down – anyway, until you get home – no, no, I don't think you should come now, we don't want to make a meal of it, she gets into enough – I mean, her reputation – much better to treat it all as – as, well, as a joke. Which is after all what it was. So – so, hang on, darling – yes, I know, I know, hang on another hour and I'll come and pick you up – yes, in an hour, on the dot, I promise – O.K. then, O.K. – oh, and give her a kiss from me. (*Puts 'phone down.*) Stupid child, stupid bloody child – oh! (*Takes off his overcoat, goes over to drinks table, pours himself a carefully measured drink, goes upstairs to study.*)

Sound of typing.

The door opens.

JASON *enters. He is dressed in tropical gear, carrying a bag. He is unshaven, almost bearded. He has his stick. He puts down bag, clutches himself, shivering, casts a glance towards the drinks table, goes to it, picks up a bottle of scotch, takes a terrific gulp. His hands are shaking. Becomes aware of the music from* MICHAEL*'s room.*

Music stops. Typing stops.

JASON *takes another quick gulp, puts bottle down. Moves away from the table, waits.*

MICHAEL *enters.*

MICHAEL (*after a shocked pause*). Japes?

JASON. Yup.

MICHAEL. Well then – Christ. (*Little laugh.*) Then you're back.

JASON. Yup.

MICHAEL. You know, I thought – I had a sudden sense that you were here, down here. I knew it. Well, let's look at you properly. (*Turns light on, goes to him, stops as if in shock at his condition, then makes to embrace him.* JASON *averts himself.*) Well – hi.

JASON. Hi.

MICHAEL. You're straight off the plane, are you, you must be – you must be – what can I get you? A drink, of course, what would you like?

JASON. Oh – have you any rum? (*Goes to sit down.*)

MICHAEL. No, sorry – almost anything else. Scotch, cognac, gin, vodka –

JASON. Whatever, scotch, I think. Yes. Scotch.

MICHAEL. Well, what does one say – a surprise, I mean – what a surprise.

JASON. To me too. I would have 'phoned, but things were a bit rushed over there, and the lines are always so bad – and at the airport – I don't understand the coins any more, I've forgotten how they work in the – the – (*Puts his arms around himself.*) slots. Telephone slots.

MICHAEL (*bringing him drink*). You're cold –

JASON. Yes, I'd forgotten that too – thank you – (*Taking drink.*) Ice. Like ice. Thank you.

MICHAEL. Shall I get you a blanket?

JASON. No, I'll be fine. More a matter of internal adjustment. (*Takes a controlled gulp.*) That's better. Soon get the heat – nothing on the plane, you see.

MICHAEL. Nothing?

JASON. Nothing.

MICHAEL. So you haven't eaten then either – all the way from Guyana here – you must be famished, let's go to the kitchen.

JASON. Oh, there was food. Food and water. And the usual rubbish. But nothing like this. No rum. Condition of travel, you see. For me anyway. All alcohol forbidden. (*Laughs.*) They filled me with pills instead. And an injection.

MICHAEL. Well, is it safe yet?

JASON (*who drinks and refills steadily from now on*). Mmm?

MICHAEL. Should you be having one now? A drink.

JASON. Oh, yes. Well, must be because I am, aren't I? (*Lifts his glass to* MICHAEL, *laughs.*) Mychy!

MICHAEL. What sort of pills? Injection? What for?

JASON. Mmmm.

MICHAEL. Are you ill then?

JASON. Ill?

MICHAEL. If they gave you pills and an injection –

JASON. Oh, just to stop me wanting a drink. Didn't work though. God, I gave them a bad time. (*Laughs.*) Shouted abuse, claimed my rights, made threats – that sort of thing. Very unattractive. But that didn't work either. Had me sort of wedged in my seat and the bloody belt sort of locked somehow so I couldn't get up to do a proper job. Also woozy. No balance. I fell asleep just before we landed. Because of the pills. They got me out of the airport into the taxi, must have because that's where I woke up. In the taxi. Told him to come here. Couldn't think of anywhere else, Mychy.

MICHAEL. There isn't anywhere else, Japes. (*Little pause.*) So it's that bad, is it?

JASON. Oh yes, Mychy. That bad. (*Nods.*)

MICHAEL. And is that the whole trouble?

JASON. Mmm?

MICHAEL. Your stomach. It's – (*Gestures.*)

JASON. Oh, that's nothing. Nothing. Don't worry about that. (*Slapping stomach which is very bloated.*) Just liquid. That's why it's tight. Drum-tight. Not flabby. Firm. Drum-firm. Hear it?

MICHAEL. Yes. So you're O.K. otherwise. Otherwise O.K.?

JASON. Otherwise. (*Does a thumbs up.*)

MICHAEL. That's a relief. That you're not back here for your health. Are you still shivering?

JASON. Shaking. Not shivering. Shaking. Mychy?

MICHAEL. Yes.

JASON. Do you mind if I – (*Gets up, goes unsteadily to table.*) help myself – (*Taking bottle.*)

MICHAEL. No, no. Of course –

JASON. I'm used to having control, you see. Over my own bottle. I get worried (*Sitting down.*) if I have to depend on other people. I've come to hate dependence. Need to cope for myself. In the university bar I have my own bottle. It's got my own name on it. And at Angry Annie's too.

MICHAEL. Angry Annie's?

JASON. Brute of a woman. Vile temper. Six children. Says two of them are mine. Don't think so, somehow. Somehow don't think so. Wrong colour. Though you never know, do you, whose child is whose, by what evidence. How is she?

MICHAEL (*after a little pause*). How is who?

JASON. Our girl of course.

MICHAEL. Ah. She's at a school party. It's a fancy dress. She's gone as a wolf.

JASON. A wolf!

MICHAEL. Yes.

JASON. Neets as a wolf! Grrrr! What a thought! Little Red Riding Wolf, eh, is that it? I can see that. Yes. Quite clearly. Little Red Neets, gone as a riding wolf.

MICHAEL. Wendy. It's Wendy that's gone as the wolf.

JASON. Wendy! Oh yes, of course, our daughter. Quite the terror, isn't she? Quite the terror.

MICHAEL. Perhaps when you last saw her. I seem to remember she was going through an odd little phase – but she was only three. She's eleven now.

JASON. Four.

MICHAEL. She's eleven, Japes.

JASON. She wasn't eleven, she wasn't three, she was four when I last saw her, Mychy. That Christmas. When we had that little what's-it over Neets. Almost fisticuffs. (*Laughs, wags his fists.*)

MICHAEL. Over Neets? No, we never had a what's-it over Neets, Japes. Though there was a disagreement over Weedon, I seem to recall.

JASON. She used to write to me a lot. Sometimes several times a week.

MICHAEL. Did she?

JASON. You knew that, didn't you?

MICHAEL. Well, that she wrote, yes, of course I did.

JASON. Some of them were a bit mad, frankly, Mychy.

MICHAEL. Were they. Well, that's very much in the past, she's working very hard on her book, her children's book, her bedbugs. The illustrations are going to be enchanting.

JASON. One-two-oops a daisy – one-two-oops-a-daisy, eh, Mychy? (*Laughs lewdly.*)

MICHAEL. How's the cold?

JASON. Still here. (*Taps chest.*) Can't get to it.

MICHAEL. I think – I think you're in a bad way, Japes. Aren't you?

JASON. What happened to the dog?

MICHAEL. Dog? Oh, wolf, you're thinking of Wendy –

JASON. No, Sandy. I'm thinking of Sandy. A labrador. Yours and mine, Mychy.

MICHAEL. Oh yes, Sandy. We had him put down – Daddy did – he had distemper.

JASON. That's it, that's right, running around in circles, foaming, we thought it was funny, didn't we, Mychy, until Mummy started screaming, wasn't rabid, though, like me.

MICHAEL. Rabid? Japes, you're not – you haven't been bitten – bitten by a dog in Guyana?

JASON *stares back at him.*

MICHAEL. Christ, Japes, well, what have they done, have they given you those shots – is that the injection?

JASON. What?

MICHAEL. You said you'd been bitten by a rabid dog.

JASON. Yes, yes, the Dean – rabid Dean – and the rest of them, the whole pack of them, whole pack of rabids coming at me – grrr! Grrr! (*Roaring, yelping, slobbering.*)

MICHAEL. Oh – oh, I see. A figure of speech. (*Gives a little laugh.*) Well, what were they coming after you for?

JASON *picks up bottle, cradles it in his lap, closes his eyes.*

MICHAEL (*looks at him*). Oh, Christ, Japes. (*To himself.*) Japes, do you know where you are? Japes. (*Goes to him, touches him on the shoulder.*) Japes. I think you need help. Or anyway to lie down, Japes. Old Japes.

JASON (*takes his hand, holds it*). Sweet Mychy. You're very sweet. (*Kisses* MICHAEL*'s hand.*) There. I'll be all right. I need to talk to you. Sit down, you're looming again, just the way I always think of you. Go on, Mychy, sit. Please. (*Suddenly roaring.*) Sit, I said!

MICHAEL *sits.*

JASON. Thank you.

MICHAEL. Can you tell me what happened?

JASON. Mmm?

MICHAEL. Well, why you're here suddenly. It's the middle of the term, isn't it? (*Little pause.*) Why did they come after you? What did you do, Japes?

JASON. Christ, Mychy, those reviews you get – I see all of them, always, in the common room, they come late of course, still reading one batch of reviews and there's another novel plopping out, and then while I'm on the reviews of that out plops another novel, and another and another, plop, plop, plop – Christ, I'm proud of you, Mychy, boast about you all over Guyana, made you big in Guyana, what was it you've got, Daddy got too, a C.B.O., is it?

MICHAEL. An O.B.E.

JASON. And perhaps a knighthood like Daddy, Sir Mychy Cartts – Sir Mychy and Lady Neets Cartts, do you think she'd like that? I would. Wouldn't mind being Lady Neets Cartts myself – (*Laughs. Begins to choke slightly, then gags hideously.*) Sorry, Mychy. Sorry. (*Little pause.*) Gets like that, you see. At a certain point. It's the blood. Bad blood. Black. That's why they've sent me to you. Because of the bad, black blood. That's what they say. But it's not the real reason. The real reason is politics. Politics and women. Americans. Three of them. Doing a tour. A tour of Caribbean us. Us.

MICHAEL. Universities?

JASON. Us. Us. Us! (*Slapping his chest.*) In the common room. My common room. On their arses. With their grants. Their doctorates. Their publications. Their – their – feminist – feminist – one of them in my chair. Everybody knew it was my chair. My bum shaped it, term in, term out, gave the cushion its – its – depth, its meaning, its value, my bum did. My bum. That's the point, Mychy, it was my bum, my chair.

MICHAEL. I see. And so you were offensive, was that it?

JASON. Polite. I was extremely polite, Herman. (*Nods, falls silent.*)

MICHAEL. Herman?

JASON. Herman?

MICHAEL. You called me Herman.

JASON. Oh. No, he's dead. One of the friendly dead. Australian geologist. I'll probably visit him in Sydney.

MICHAEL. Please, Japes, you should lie down.

JASON. Why?

MICHAEL. Because you're drunk, Japes. Exhausted. And I don't want Anita and Wendy to see you – Wendy in particular – you wouldn't want her to, either.

JASON. Sitting on their arses in my chair in my common room – *my* common room – 'What would you three ladies like to drink?' Don't call us ladies, very offensive, to be called ladies, and I said, what then, what do I call you, and they said anything, anything but ladies, so I said, 'Right then, right, what can I get you three cunts' (*Begins to laugh.*) – cunts, I called them cunts – 'what would you three cunts' – and then I took it out – (*Stands up, swaying, unzips his flies, gropes for his penis.*) 'Here, cunts, have a look at this, have a look at this!'

MICHAEL. Yes, Japes, all right, (*Putting his hand preventively on* JASON*'s arm.*) I get the – the –

JASON. I keep my pension though.

MICHAEL. Japes – Japes – come along, Japes, come along. (*Attempting to take* JASON*'s arm.*)

JASON (*pulling violently away*). You listen to me, Mychy, you listen to me. This is my house, half this is my house, you can't throw me out of it, Mychy, you can't keep me away from it – I own half and I want it. I've come back for it. I'm taking it and I'm taking my half of everything else, Mychy. My half of the daughter, my half of the wife, the half that belongs to me. Do you understand, Mychy? Understand it?

MICHAEL. Yes, of course, Japes. You'll have everything that belongs to you. Of course you will.

JASON. Just half, Mychy, just my half. No more, no less, just my half.

MICHAEL. Yes – yes, just your half. Now will you come with me and lie down? Just for a while. Just for a little while. When you wake up, there'll be Neets and there'll be Wendy, and I'll be there. And you'll be in your family again.

JASON. My family again. Oh, Mychy, my family again – oh, Mychy – oh, Mychy – (*Holds his arms out, lurching.*)

As MICHAEL *goes to him,* JASON *reels away and collapses to the floor. He is making retching sounds, goes still as death, face turned up.*

MICHAEL *goes to him, takes him in his arms, cradles him.*

MICHAEL. Oh, Japes, my Japes – (*Lets out an animal howl of grief.*)

Lights.

Curtain.

ACT TWO

Scene One

Five years later.

There is a student's briefcase on the floor, contents, including purse and keys, scattered about. Also some papers, books. A transistor is lying on the floor, playing popular music, loudly. The television is on.

ANITA *is sprawled on the sofa, drinking a glass of wine. She has a bottle beside her, has already had a few glasses. Also beside her a drawing pad, a case of pencils, etc.*

There is a ring at the doorbell.

ANITA *registers it, looks towards door. Front door opens, off.*

JASON *enters. He is carrying a carrier bag. He uses a different, up-to-date stick, walks more easily.*

JASON. Hi. (*Then raising his voice.*) Hi!

ANITA. Hi!

JASON. May I make some silence?

ANITA. What?

JASON. Turn things off.

ANITA. Oh, yes, yes. I'd almost stopped noticing.

JASON *turns off television set, goes to turn off transistor.*

JASON (*fiddling with transistor*). I don't know how you do these bloody –

ANITA. Oh, just smash it to death is what I long to do – but this is what I usually do. (*Puts bottle down, takes it, opens the back, shakes out batteries.*) Hi, Japes.

JASON. Hi, Neets.

ANITA. Thanks for coming round.

JASON. Well, you sounded – you sounded desperate on the 'phone.

ANITA. Sorry, I was in a state. Actually, I still am. We just had the most terrible row – the most terrible bloody awful row – about this (*Shaking transistor.*) being on, and that (*Pointing at television with transistor.*) being on, and then she went off and I've been sitting here, with them still on, not even hearing, what do you make of that, Japes, eh?

JASON. Oh, referred something or other, isn't it called, these days. You know, if you have a pain in your leg, it's actually being referred there from your neck – so if you have a row about noise and then don't do anything about the noise, it's really a referred row – or something. In other words, I can't make anything of it.

ANITA (*picking up bag, wallet, keys, etc.*). She's left home for good. Without her keys, her money – (*Putting them into bag.*) oh, and her pot and stuff, so she'll be back, won't she, though will it be for good or for ill, will she be back for good or for ill is the question? What can I get you, tea, coffee, squash –

JASON. I've brought my own. (*Taking bottle out of bag.*) Saw it in that new health shop in the village, the one with jars of weeds and turds and what have you in the window – and there was this – herbal – costs about three times as much as a bottle of wine – but then I suppose you're meant to keep the bottle to put weeds and turds in –

ANITA (*bringing him glass*). I went out to draw, you see. That turned out to be my mistake.

JASON. Oh. (*Pouring himself a drink.*)

ANITA (*filling her glass from wine*). Such a beautiful day. And suddenly there was the impulse – it's been years, Japes, honestly, years –

JASON. Yes, yes, it must be.

ANITA. So. So I was very careful. Thoughtful. Dutiful. Reminded her that her half-term was over tomorrow and she still hadn't gone to the library to do her project on – on – some history, King Charles the one of them, the one that lost his head I think it was – and I was very sweet, I really was, knocked on her door, said, 'Darling, isn't it time you were off?', gave her a couple of quid for her tea – hah, hah! – and said we'd see her for dinner, eating a bit late because of Daddy, about eight-thirty, that all right, darling, all right, darling? (*Smiles ingratiatingly at* JASON.)

JASON *laughs.*

So then I went and sorted out my things, one ear cocked, you know, to make sure she'd actually gone, and then I heard the door open and close and – and off I went, with my pad and my pencils, to St Mark's as a matter of fact, back to my early period, my only period – remember when I used to draw it all the time back then? – and anyway, I didn't, I suddenly couldn't, didn't want my pad or my pencils sitting in the sun trying to do something that it would just make me miserable and resentful not being able to do so came back to the house to find her here, also back in the house, lying on this – (*Indicating sofa.*) dragging on a joint, with her bloody noise, and it was the – the thought of it, I mean, that she must have loitered about around the corner in the street or something until she'd seen me gone, and then come back and – the television and the tranny and the pot and the whole slatternly, slovenly, rubbishy – and so I went for her, and she went for me – and – (*Gestures.*) well no, that's not fair, not fair on me. I tried to do the grown-up crap first, you know, very calm, cold and calm and reasonable, and she grunted, and smirked and sneered – so I got Mychy into it – 'remember what your father said about kindness, the real meaning of the word' – then I couldn't remember what he said the real meaning of the word was, it was all very complicated, being Mychy – and anyway, anyway, she just sat there, her eyes deliberately glazed and lips – that way she does – (*Pushes her lips out.*) and that's when I – I hit her, Japes. The thing is – (*Begins to cry.*)

JASON. Oh, Neets. (*Goes to her, puts an arm around her.*)

ANITA. Across the face. Like a punch. A punch. Oh Christ, Japes.

JASON. It's O.K., it's O.K. – it'll be all right, you'll see, you'll see.

ANITA. I wanted to go after her – I wanted to go after her – I really did, but – but –

JASON. She'll be back. You'll make it all right. You know, she's not – not bad or anything –

ANITA. Well, I'm not bad either.

JASON. No, of course you're not. You're both good, very good and – and kind actually.

ANITA. Then why are we so bad, so unkind with each other.

JASON. Well, perhaps because you're both more like each other than either of you recognises, eh, Neets? Sometimes when I'm with one of you it's as if I'm with the other, I forget which is which – the same gestures, even the same sort of jokes, you know.

ANITA. Jokes? She makes jokes with you, does she? How often do you actually see her, Japes?

JASON. Well, only during her holidays. And even then she's usually away, on school trips or somewhere else, isn't she?

ANITA. Yes, but when she is here, like now, how often do you see her?

JASON. Well, she looks in now and then.

ANITA. At your flat?

JASON. Of course at my flat, Neets. It's no secret – at least I've never made a secret of it.

ANITA. But perhaps you don't always say, either.

JASON. Well, if I don't, it's not deliberately. Why? Do you mind?

ANITA. Well, what do you joke about? What sort of things do you talk about together, in your flat?

JASON. Well, whatever comes up. Whatever's on her mind.

ANITA. Oh. Like her shrink, you mean?

JASON. Well, no, not like her shrink. For one thing, I don't charge, you see.

ANITA. Do you talk about us?

JASON. Which us?

ANITA. Any two or three of us. Well, do you?

JASON. Really, Neets, I've said, she just pops in now and then, and if I'm busy trying to finish an article or don't feel in the mood, I chuck her out, virtually. It's like that, you see.

ANITA. I suppose I sound jealous, do I?

JASON. No, you just sound as if you regret having to be a mother when you'd like to be a friend.

ANITA. Was that on purpose?

JASON. Mmm?

ANITA. Did you misunderstand me on purpose? I didn't mean jealous of you with her, I mean the other way around.

JASON. Then I did misunderstand you, yes. What I love in her is you.

ANITA. Thank you. That's lovely. Thank you. (*Kisses him.*) You're still tops at that sort of thing, Japes. What a gift. But if you love me in her, why don't I love me in her, too? I mean, if I hate myself, does that mean that I hate her.

JASON. You don't hate her.

ANITA. I do sometimes. Yes.

JASON. No. You get angry –

ANITA. No, of course I don't hate her. Why did I say that? It's anger – of course it's anger. And it's with myself really, you're right about that too, and it probably all comes down to my being frightened.

JASON. Frightened?

ANITA. Well, I'm at that age, you know – it does happen – I could go menopausal any minute, I could be menopausal now, which would explain me a bit, my ups and downs and downs and ups. (*Pours herself more wine.*)

JASON. Darling –

ANITA. Mmmm?

JASON. Darling, Neets. (*Shakes his head.*)

ANITA. Am I drunk?

JASON. Well, you soon will be.

ANITA. And you wouldn't want to see her see me drunk, is that it?

JASON. I don't want to see you drunk. And you always hate it afterwards.

ANITA. You talk as if I do it all the time.

JASON. You've done it once or twice recently.

ANITA. But only with you. Well, mainly only with you. Only sometimes with poor Mychy, he hates it so much – especially if she's around, so never when she's around, honestly, Japes.

JASON. I know, Neets. Where is Mychy?

ANITA. He's doing one of his things, one of his television things. A very, very big one this time.

JASON. Oh yes, of course. Writers of Our Time.

ANITA. It's going to make him even more famous. Which means he'll come home all humble and depressed. Isn't it funny how it depresses him – you'd have loved it, success and fame – perhaps you should each of you have been the other – but then would I have liked that because then he'd have been here and you'd have been there, being interviewed – would you have liked it that way round, Japes, that's the question, would you, Japes darling? (*Sees* JASON*'s expression.*) Oh, come on, Japes, what's the matter, I'm only talking, you know me, just talking.

JASON. Just talking. I wonder why we always say that – 'just talking' when talking is about as dangerous as driving, probably ruins as many lives, if not more, really we should set out the same sort of signs – 'sharp curve in next sentence', 'unfortunate joke ahead', 'slippery surface', 'beware soft patches' –

ANITA. And as for talking under the influence – here, here you are, Japes. Uncle Japes. Take it away. (*Pushes bottle to him.*) Oh, sorry, darling, the smell, I forgot – here, I'll pour it away.

JASON. No, I'm perfectly capable. (*Turns to pick up stick.*)

As he does so, ANITA *jerks bottle away from* JASON *who stumbles, falls to his knees.*

ANITA. Oh, look, it's almost gone, I might as well – darling, are you all right?

JASON. Yes, yes, I'm fine. (*Getting up, sits down.*)

ANITA. Well then, you mustn't glower. It never suits you. Remember what you once said to me – 'at heart, you were a merry man'?

JASON. Yes. Yes, I am. You're quite right. A merry man. (*Little pause.*) So you went up to St Mark's to do a drawing?

ANITA. No, no, I didn't, I told you. I didn't have the nerve, you see.

JASON. The nerve?

ANITA. I think I'll become a friend instead. They're always pushing stuff through the letter box asking – help keep the grounds up, tend the graves, I suppose, that sort of thing – I mean, if I can't draw it again I can – I can – be its friend instead. Just like your Mummy. Yours and Mychy's Mummy, Japes.

JASON. I wish you did more drawings.

ANITA. Why? So I wouldn't be so bored and such a nuisance?

JASON. You have a talent.

ANITA. That's not what you said back then, when I was being serious and a proper student. You said the only talent I had was as pussy.

JASON. No, I didn't. (*Little pause.*) I couldn't have said that. Not ever.

ANITA. Yes, you did. (*Rubs herself against him, purring.*)

JASON. Oh! (*Laughs.*) Yes, yes – (*Strokes her head.*) Well, that's all right then, because it's true – except it wasn't, isn't, your only talent. You can draw. You really can. And if you really can't do St Mark's – well, what about your children's book – the woodlice, wasn't it going to be – why don't you get back to that, Neets?

ANITA. Bedbugs actually. Basil and Archie, the Bashful Bedbugs. I burnt them.

JASON. Burnt them?

ANITA. My Bedbugs.

JASON. Why?

ANITA. You wouldn't understand. Mychy didn't. Why should you?

JASON. Well, you might give me the chance at least.

There is a pause.

JASON. Why did you burn your Bedbugs, Neets?

ANITA. Because when you came back in that dreadful state and nearly died on us – on me – when you were in intensive care and were almost gone for ever for three whole days – I made a deal. You see?

JASON. A deal? What sort of deal, with whom?

ANITA. How would I know? But I called him God. I made a deal with – with the God one makes deals with. Up at St Mark's, as a matter of fact. I wanted to do it inside, on a pew, but the doors were locked, so I did it in the churchyard. I said it aloud, at eleven thirty-seven on the Wednesday night of April the thirteenth. Straight after seeing you lying there dead, as good as, as good as dead.

JASON. That if I lived you'd – you'd –

ANITA. Well, it's the only thing I cared – really cared about that I could renounce, wasn't it? I mean I couldn't renounce Mychy or Wendy, could I, all I had to offer was my Bedbugs.

JASON. Thank you. But Neets, my darling Neets, it's over, my illness, and I'm here, and you've got a life to live, a talent – look, Neets, what really brought me back was a life support machine, an exceptionally capable liver specialist called Sapperstein, and just possibly – just possibly – my own will to live. (*Little pause.*) Can't you see what a burden you're putting on me by making me somehow responsible – without even giving me a say in the matter. I would never have been party to such a deal –

ANITA. Can we stop this now, please, Japes? It's making me feel sick. It's quite simple, quite simple. If you'd died I'd have been lost. You've always been what's kept me going, Japes, even when you were on the other side of the world, you kept me where I am, and if you'd died – I'd have died too. Been dead too – for them. (*Pause.*) And that's all there is to it, all right? All right, Japes?

JASON. Of course it's all right. After all, it's not much of a burden, is it, being responsible for your abandoning your talent so that you can keep the family afloat.

ANITA. Well, we all have our part to play, don't we? I have to be the wife and mother, and whatever you think and whatever you and Mychy think and whatever you and Mychy and the daughter think, at least I try most of the time, and if I have a rotten afternoon sometimes and ask you to come around – well, I still don't ask for much from you, do I? All things considered, do I?

JASON, *after a little pause, shakes his head.*

ANITA. So you can go if you want. I'm all right now.

JASON. I don't want to go.

ANITA. Haven't you got any work to do? You're always saying you've got work to do – all those articles on all those poets in all those magazines – I wish I could read them, I would if I could understand them – funny how I can always understand what Mychy writes, but then he's popular, isn't he, and that's why – that's why he's – (*Gestures.*) and you're – (*Gestures.*)

JASON. Oh, Neets, oh God, Neets! (*Half laughing.*)

ANITA. You think I'm going to do some more drinking.

JASON. I hope not. Please don't. For my sake.

ANITA. Do I make you want to drink, then?

JASON. Not always. But occasionally, when you're like this, I feel an urge to join in.

ANITA. For old times' sake?

JASON. Well, there are only old times because suddenly there are new times.

ANITA. Really? Really, really, really. New times are afoot, are they, at last, at long last.

JASON. I mean – I'm staying for your sake. For everybody's sake. And you're not going to drink for my sake. And that's it, Neets.

ANITA. My jailer then, is what you plan to be, is it? I think I'll open another bottle and see what happens. (*Heads towards kitchen.*)

JASON *hesitates, makes a decision, heads towards door.*

ANITA (*re-emerging*). Or you can do me a poem. (*Goes to sofa, sits, pats sofa.*) Come on, I promise I'll be good.

JASON, *after a moment, goes to sofa, sits down.*

ANITA *moves closer to him.*

ANITA. Go on then.

JASON.
Slowly the poison the whole blood stream fills.
It is not the effort nor the failure tires.
The waste remains, the waste remains and kills.

It is not your system of clear sight that mills
Down small to the consequence a life requires;
Slowly the poison the whole blood stream fills.

They bled an old dog dry –

ANITA. Stop it, Japes! That's not poetry, it's cruelty! Old dog! Poison! You're making it up to punish me.

JASON. No, I'm not. And it's a poem all right. It's called 'Missing Dates'. I use it as an *aide memoire.*

ANITA. Do that one – that one – the crying girl one. Simple and faithless – 'La Figlia che – La Figlia che' –

JASON. 'La Figlia che Piange'.

ANITA. 'La Figlia che Piange'. (*Arranges herself, with her head on his lap.*)

JASON.
Stand on the highest pavement of the stair
Lean on a garden urn
Weave, weave the sunlight in your hair-
Clasp your flowers to you with a pained surprise –
Fling them to the ground and turn
With a fugitive resentment in your eyes:
But weave, weave the sunlight in your hair.

ANITA *and* JASON *kiss passionately.*

ANITA. Got you again. Haven't I? Got you. Got you. Got you.

JASON. Yes, oh, Neets, Neets, yes.

Lights begin to go down as ANITA *and* JASON *make love passionately.*

Lights up on JASON *and* ANITA *lying with her head in his lap, both asleep.*

Sound of door opening.

MICHAEL (*off*). Hi, anybody.

MICHAEL *enters, looks at them, arranges* ANITA*'s clothing, picks up knickers and stuffs them into his pocket. He goes to adjust* JASON*'s clothing.*

JASON *is murmuring lines from 'La Figlia che Piange' in his sleep.*

MICHAEL *attempts to zip up* JASON*'S fly.*

JASON *feels* MICHAEL*'s hand on him, clutches it as he wakes up, stares at* MICHAEL.

MICHAEL. Cogitations. It's cogitations. Not meditations.

JASON. What?

MICHAEL. 'La Figlia che Piange'. You were reciting it in your sleep. But you said 'these meditations still surprise', instead of 'these cogitations still surprise' –

JASON. Oh. Yes, 'cogitations'. But 'amaze', isn't it? 'These cogitations still amaze' –

MICHAEL. 'Amaze'! Yes, you're right. 'Amaze'. 'These cogitations still amaze / The troubled midnight' – two completely different conditions, really, 'surprise' being a kind of shock to the system, a being taken out of, while 'amaze' is – a growing, a growing sense of – (*Gestures.*) oh, where's Wendy?

JASON. Actually, she's at my place. Or was the last time I saw her. She turned up suddenly, in a bit of a state, she'd had a spat with – (*Nods.*) you see, and – so forth.

MICHAEL. Oh. What about, did she say?

JASON. No, well, before she could get into it properly –

ANITA (*moving in sleep*). Japes, Japes –

JASON (*nods at* ANITA). 'Phoned, and asked me to come over, so I got her version instead. As far as I could make out it was to do with transistors being on, television being on, school projects not being attended to – anyway she's still in my flat, our Wendy, or was when last seen.

ANITA (*moans out in her sleep*). No – no – (*Mumblingly.*) Mychy –

JASON. I think it's for you.

MICHAEL. Ah. There, there, darling. There, there, I'm here. (*Going to her, patting her gently.*) She's such a – such a lovely – when she's asleep. This little frown, have you noticed?

JASON. Yes. Actually, my good leg's going – do you think you could –

MICHAEL. Oh, right, here. (*Takes* JASON*'s place, except with his arm around her shoulder.*) Goodness, she's gone again, isn't she? Completely out. Would you mind –

JASON *takes* MICHAEL*'s glass, pours scotch into it. As he does so, takes a quick sniff at the drink, feels it deep in his soul, brings glass back to* MICHAEL.

MICHAEL. Do you think I should get her to bed? Well, what else did you talk about, the two of you, apart from the usual Wendy?

JASON. I can't really remember – oh, yes, I asked her about her children's book –

MICHAEL. Bedbugs! She talked about her bedbugs, did she? Well, that's good, being able to talk about it means she must be getting over it at last, the humiliation of it. Poor old Neets. (*Strokes her cheek.*)

JASON. Humiliation?

MICHAEL. Well, (*Checking to make sure* ANITA*'s still gone, lowering his voice slightly.*) that's what she saw it as, failure and humiliation, although Weedon claimed he never actually rejected it outright – the worst he'd been was mildly discouraging, according to him, but the fact is that whatever he said, he completely undermined her confidence. Did she tell you about what she did with them, her Bedbugs?

JASON. She said she'd burnt them.

MICHAEL. Burnt them? Is that what she told you? No, no, she didn't burn them, she taxied drunkenly home from her lunch with Weedon, and tried to flush them down the lavatory. I found her up to her ankles in water, pulling away at the chain, sobbing and screaming out, well, curses really, curses on Weedon, on her bedbugs, on everything, everyone, all of us, her whole life – since then, she's refused to discuss them, gets quite hysterical when I mention them – but if she's started with you – that could be a good sign, she might be thinking of getting down to them again, eh? But as for Weedon – what was it you called him once – oh, yes – fuckwit. He's a complete fuckwit. You should have heard him this afternoon. After that interview. But then I shouldn't have agreed to do it, should I? My own fault entirely. I let him bully me into it. So it's because of him that next month there I'll be, in a million homes, think of it, a million and a half, actually, dilating on the theme of my fictions, the recurrent themes, like recurrent colds or sore throats or prison sentences – no, that's concurrent, isn't it – anyway, loss, loss and betrayal, my recurrent themes, with an occasional whiff of redemption, he could sniff it, he said, sniff the whiff of redemption on my prose. On my latest prose. But actually I don't think it's redemption, more an acceptance, an informed acceptance of the nature of things.

JASON. Mychy, I think I'd better go.

MICHAEL. Could you give us a hand, just to get her to her feet.

JASON. No, I mean go away. I've been thinking of it for quite a while now. Of going away for a bit.

MICHAEL (*after a little pause*). How long a bit?

JASON. I don't know. For quite a bit, I expect.

MICHAEL. Well, not for good, you don't mean? (*Little pause.*) But where would you go? Not back to Guyana, for God's sake! I won't allow it, Japes.

JASON. No, nowhere warm, don't worry. In fact I wouldn't mind trying somewhere really cold. Icy even. With stiff winds. Might get me back to some real writing again, a hostile climate. Do we know anything about Nova Scotia?

MICHAEL. Nova Scotia? Canada. East coast. Near where the Titanic went down. You'd hate it. Look, Japes, what I've really been trying to say – don't you understand what I'm trying to say – that it's all right, you see. It really is.

JASON. What is?

MICHAEL. I don't mind. That's what I'm saying. I don't mind.

JASON. Don't mind what?

MICHAEL. That you've started again. (*Little pause.*) I mean, here we are, we've reached this stage of – of, well, our lives with each other. These could be good years, good years, why shouldn't they be? Here. Together. As we used to be, but – but grown up. A little grown up anyway. That's the point, Japes. (*Little pause.*) We need you, is also the point. She needs you. Desperately needs you. As do I. Is the point.

JASON. But it's time I learnt not to need you, either of you is the point, Mychy, for me. I've got to go. You see.

ANITA (*waking up*). Mychy, Mychy. (*Looking vaguely towards* JASON.)

MICHAEL. Actually, I'm here, Neets.

ANITA. Oh. Oh, so you are. I knew you were, the two of you, I could hear your voices winding about in my sleep, well, what's been going on? (*Getting up shakily.*) What have you been talking about?

MICHAEL. Actually, Japes has just been saying that he's going away.

ANITA. Going away?

MICHAEL. To Nova Scotia, he thinks.

ANITA. Nova Scotia.

JASON. It's near where the Titanic went down.

There is a ring on the doorbell.

MICHAEL. Who the hell is that?

JASON. Wendy, isn't it? She forgot her keys, didn't you say?

MICHAEL. Oh. Well, I'll go and – and (*Goes to door, off.*)

JASON *and* ANITA *look at each other.* JASON *turns away, picks up* MICHAEL*'s drink, lifts it.*

WENDY (*voice off, inaudible*).

MICHAEL (*off*). Don't be silly, darling, of course we want you, come in.

JASON *puts the glass down firmly, looks at* ANITA.

ANITA. You can't.

MICHAEL (*off*). Oh, for heaven's sake, Wendy, nobody's going to eat you, I promise!

ANITA. I won't let you.

Lights.

Scene Two

Ten years later.

Lights up on empty room. Graffiti on the wall, furniture spilled, etc. Sound of door opening, off. MICHAEL *enters. Takes in shambles, then takes in the graffiti. Looks around, then goes to door as if to check on other rooms. Becomes aware of sounds off, another presence in the house. Stands uncertain and alarmed, then goes to telephone, dials.*

WENDY *enters as from other rooms.*

MICHAEL. Neets. (*Staring at her.*)

WENDY. No, Dad. Not Neets.

MICHAEL. Wendy? (*Then recognising her.*) Good heavens, yes, it's Wendy. Well – well, Wendy. (*Takes in shambles.*)

WENDY. Yes, sorry about this.

MICHAEL. No, no, not at all, that's all right. (*Little pause.*) Um, what happened?

WENDY. Well, a fit of pique, I suppose it was.

MICHAEL. Ah. You had a fit of pique. Well –

WENDY. Not mine, actually. The bloke I was with.

MICHAEL. Oh. He wasn't by any chance a youngish man, in an orangish coat and a bit of a beard?

WENDY. Dark hair? Long dark hair?

MICHAEL. Yes, yes, definitely darkish. He passed me on the other side of the street just a moment ago, I thought he might have come out of the house. Shouted out to me. My name. Well, I suppose my name. 'Hello there, Sir Michael, all well, Sir Michael?' And then he laughed. And gestured rather – obscenely as a matter of fact.

WENDY. Yes, that was him all right. His name's Dominic. He's a recovering junkie, and like me he's still a bit fragile in some ways. He suddenly took it into his head that you'd despise him when you saw him, so he did this as a way of getting back at you. It's called 'inferiority rage' one of his shrinks said, it only comes in situations where he feels inferior – but I probably don't have to apologise for him, by now he'll be looking forward to doing it for himself.

MICHAEL. Oh, tell him there's really no need, no need –

WENDY. Well, you'll probably be meeting him some time because he's responsible for this. (*Patting her stomach.*)

MICHAEL. Mmm?

WENDY. I'm pregnant, Dad.

MICHAEL. Oh, I noticed you'd filled out, I thought it might be that, I nearly mentioned it but sometimes you know one makes a mistake. And then it can be rather embarrassing.

WENDY. A friend of mine had a tumour there. And of course everybody assumed she was pregnant. She found it rather – embarrassing.

MICHAEL. I'm sure she did, I'm sure she did. A tumour. (*Little pause.*)

WENDY. You look older.

MICHAEL. Well, yes. But then I am.

WENDY. No, I mean older than I expected. Elderly. You look almost elderly.

MICHAEL. Do I? Well, it's been some years since you last saw me after all. Quite a few years it must be.

WENDY. Seven years.

MICHAEL. Is that it? Really? Well, there you are. Would you like something? A – a – well, I don't know, what would you like, anything?

WENDY. No, thanks. But if you want something –

MICHAEL. No, no, well, perhaps just a – (*Goes over, pours himself a drink.*) I could do with this.

WENDY. Yes, I mean coming back and finding your house vandalised and your long-gone daughter standing there pregnant by the vandal must be a bit of a shock. Sorry, Dad, perhaps I should have given you a bit of warning.

MICHAEL. No, no, it's wonderful having you just – just – how did you get in?

WENDY. I hung on to my key, the one thing I didn't let go of. And you hadn't changed the locks. In fact you don't seem to have changed anything very much, have you?

MICHAEL. No, I suppose I haven't.

WENDY. So what's it like to be a grand-daddy, Dad? I expect you'll be pleased to help out the way that grand-daddies do.

MICHAEL. Well – yes, I will if I can. Of course I will.

WENDY. Thank you. I could always count on your kindness, couldn't I, Dad?

MICHAEL. My kindness?

WENDY. I remember your little lecture on kindness. Kith, kin, kindness in nature, remember?

MICHAEL. Yes.

WENDY. And how it had turned itself into a dead word. No sense of responsibility. No tribal significance.

MICHAEL. Well, that's frequently the way with words, the important ones, they come away from their stems, drift about like – like petals, into the breeze of this conversation and that – decorative and useless.

WENDY. Where have you been?

MICHAEL. Mmm?

WENDY. Just now, where have you come from?

MICHAEL. Oh, um, the Garrick. I lunch there most days – these days.

WENDY. Ah. I thought you might have been up to the church.

MICHAEL. The church?

WENDY. Yes, Mum's church, up the road.

MICHAEL. Oh, St Mark's, yes – no, no, I was at the Garrick.

WENDY. She's there, though, isn't she?

MICHAEL. What? Oh, at St Mark's. No, no, I tried of course, but they ran out of room a long time ago – even for 'Friends'. I do walk up there, though, now and then. For the walk and the fresh air and of course –

WENDY. Well, where is she then?

MICHAEL. Golders Green. It turned out to be the nearest, the most convenient.

WENDY. And is that where Japes is too? Beside her?

MICHAEL. Yes. Well, no. One down as a matter of fact. The plot next to hers had already been taken. By someone called Tuffins. Joseph Tuffins. There was a misunderstanding with the undertakers. I asked for a space in between, meaning to reserve it for myself, but instead of leaving an empty space they left a full one. Full of Tuffins – Joseph Tuffins – died March 13 1984. If you're thinking of visiting I can let you have their numbers. The numbers of their graves. It can be very confusing at Golders Green.

WENDY. Did you have a joint funeral then?

MICHAEL. Yes.

WENDY. Is that usual?

MICHAEL. Not for me. But then it was a first, wasn't it? I wrote to you about it. I didn't know quite where to get hold of you so I sent it to the clinic – your last address, as known to me, hoping they'd send it on. Did it find you?

WENDY. No. Well – it may have done but it wouldn't have mattered, I wasn't opening envelopes at that time. Particularly if they had familiar handwriting on them.

MICHAEL. Still, you seem to know all about it.

WENDY. Dominic came across something in the newspapers – actually he ended up with quite a pile of clippings. he kept them for me so I'd have news from home when I got out of prison.

MICHAEL. Were you in for long?

WENDY. A few months. Five actually.

MICHAEL. It was something to do with drugs, I assume.

WENDY. No, fraud actually. I got hold of someone's credit card – although you're right really, it's what they classify as a drugs-related crime when they make up those lists of drugs-related crimes. Anyway, everything I bought fraudulently, I sold for drugs. Did they do it on purpose?

Little pause.

WENDY. Well, some of the newspapers hinted at it. That they committed suicide or even one of them had murdered the other and then –

MICHAEL. It was a simple act of carelessness. They were both careless, you know, in their way – especially when they were – when they were – together. They simply fell asleep, not noticing that the place was filling with fumes from that damn French heating. (*Little pause.*) They were naked on top of the sheets which proves – well, according to the French – that it wouldn't have been suicide or – or – it's characteristic of suicides to present themselves respectably, comme il faut – and there were two empty bottles of Calvados by the bed so they'd also been drinking very heavily – but there was nothing unusual about that, no, no, it was those fumes, those French fumes, that did it.

WENDY. Japes drinking? But the last time I saw him he'd stopped forever.

MICHAEL. Alcoholics do that regularly, don't they? Anyway, he chose to move to Antibes, a legendary place for drunks. Graham Greene, you know.

WENDY. And Mum, I know she drank a bit but are you saying she become an alcoholic?

MICHAEL. She was drinking quite a lot, and taking pills.

WENDY. I don't suppose it was because of me, my disappearing like that.

MICHAEL. No, no, you mustn't blame yourself, Wendy, you didn't come into it. She had a hard time, you know, with the menopause. And then my attempt to get her back to her Bedbugs, you remember them, those delightful illustrations, it rather backfired, she became obsessed with my agent, my then agent, Weedon, of course you knew him, didn't you, from when you were a child, she embarked on a vendetta against him, threatening 'phone calls, visits to his office, waylaying him in restaurants, accusing him of ruining her life, it all became very messy, fortunately Weedon was very understanding, although he had to get a restraining order – and then there were the pills, she managed to get herself prescribed all sorts of pills, anti-depressants, pro-depressants, and she went back to smoking a lot of – of – (*Nods vaguely to* WENDY.) all this along with the drinking. I had to leave Weedon, needless to say. I've got a new agent. A young man. Australian. (*Gestures.*)

WENDY. But you didn't think of getting her into a clinic?

MICHAEL. Of course I did, but she wouldn't consider it.

WENDY. I wouldn't consider it either but I seemed to find myself in one anyway.

MICHAEL. It was different with you. You were still at an age.

WENDY. Was she living with Japes?

MICHAEL. Living with him?

WENDY. Had she left you to live with him?

MICHAEL. Well, not to my knowledge.

WENDY. Not to your knowledge!

MICHAEL. Well, she came to my door. Upstairs. My study door. She knocked. She came in. She said she was going. She was wearing a coat and a – a – she was dressed for going.

WENDY. For going to Japes?

MICHAEL. She didn't say where but then she didn't have to. I knew the content of the word, its full content. Every time she came to my door dressed for going and said she was going, I knew she was going to Antibes.

WENDY. So you expected her back then?

MICHAEL. Well, of course I expected her back. Just as I always expected her to go, I always expected her to come back.

WENDY. And you didn't mind?

MICHAEL. On the contrary. I was pleased she had something to look forward to. Both coming and going.

WENDY. What about their wills?

MICHAEL. Their wills?

WENDY. Yes. Was I left anything?

MICHAEL. Your mother and I made an elementary will just after we got married, leaving everything to each other. We never got around to anything more complicated.

WENDY. And Japes?

MICHAEL. He hadn't left a will. As I'm the next of kin what he had came to me.

WENDY. What about Mum's personal stuff, did you keep any of it?

MICHAEL. I gave her clothes to Help the Aged. I didn't know what else to do with them.

WENDY. Well, (*Little pause.*) what about her other things, her jewellery and that.

MICHAEL. I sold it.

WENDY (*after a pause*). Did you, Dad? Sold it?

MICHAEL. I sold all Japes's books and personal things too. So altogether there was quite a lot of money. I gave it to St Mark's. It seems to me that's what she would have wanted. And Japes would have wanted what she would have wanted. (*Pause.*) I had to do everything by instinct. Guess-work, anyway. After all, I had nobody to consult, did I? So all I had to go on were my instinct and my guesses. Perhaps I should have kept it for you, but then where were you, dropped out, vanished, in another country or dead too, for all I knew.

WENDY. No, it's all right, Dad. I understand how you came to do it, I really do. You wouldn't have wanted me around anyway. Far better for you to keep it between the three of you, as usual – that's what I thought when I got the news that they were dead and how they'd done it – that it was just the three of you, my Dad, my uncle, and my Mum, as usual, I didn't come into it, my proper place was in jail or wherever while all this moving and burying of their bodies and selling of their goods was going on, I'd have been in the way again, and it's not the money or the goods I think I've got a right to at last, it's far more than that, Dad. It's the rest of my life really. Beginning with my past. But then the two are connected, at least that's what my shrink says, so give me back my past, Dad, would you, please?

MICHAEL. But surely you know your past better than anyone?

WENDY. One of the things I'm coming to understand is that what one remembers about the past isn't necessarily the past.

MICHAEL. How interesting. I should have thought that's exactly what it is, the past. One's memories. What else can it be?

WENDY. But one can keep adding to it, can't one, Dad? Suddenly remembering things one had never remembered before. That suddenly makes sense of the other things one remembered but never understood.

MICHAEL. How interesting. And of course you're quite right, Wendy. One can't set limits to what one remembers, what would be the use, our memories don't honour any limits we set them, they still come at us around corners we didn't even know were there, giving us a glimpse, just a glimpse, of some *once* waiting to reveal itself – some once that once was, once – in fact, just this morning I was sitting down to write – I'm having a go at my memoirs, nothing too personal, really a sort of record of my time as I noticed it slipping towards me, around me, away from me – and those lines of Dr Johnson popped into my head, those wonderful and terrible lines on Dr Robert Levet, 'A Practiser in Physic', that always seem to me to be about me, the drudgery, the sheer drudgery of, well, of being me. 'Condemn'd to hope's delusive mine / As on we toil from day to day / By sudden blasts or slow decline / Our social comforts drop away ' – I was quite, well, surprised, I hadn't thought of them for years, but then I suddenly remembered, right back *then*, when I was writing one of my early novels, and full of vigour for it, eagerness to get at it – I'd almost rush to my study, you probably remember me, when you were little, rushing to my study, and then I'd see them, you know, the drafts – the drafts – and just the sight of them – before I actually sat down to begin – the sight of them, on the desk, in the drawers, on the floor, the wastepaper basket stuffed with discards – that was my idea of completeness, not a final draft, but a final discard – and a weariness of spirit, not of body or of concentration – no, a weariness of spirit was what it was, and I'd find myself chanting those lines to myself, 'Condemned to hope's delusive mine / As on we toil from day to day' – they'd get into my head like some ghastly ditty, I'd even type to the rhythm (*Simulates typing to the rhythm of the lines.*) and I remembered too how I'd sometimes despised Japes, that he never saw anything through, draft through draft to the final draft, and how I envied him too, that instead he could be down here, down *here* (*Gestures.*) with Neets, your mother, talking and laughing and – and with Neets, your mother, like a – proper – a proper –

WENDY. Ah yes, those years ago while you were up there, drafting on draft after draft, and Mum was down here talking with Japes, and laughing, and fucking and being fucked by him.

MICHAEL. Yes, I suppose you had to say it, didn't you? It's the – the currency of your lot, isn't it?

WENDY. My lot? (*Laughs.*)

MICHAEL. Even though you understood – you perfectly understood that I was trying in my way, the way of my lot, to tell you something. Wasn't that enough?

WENDY. The proper words for it matter, Dad. To me anyway. To my lot.

MICHAEL. They certainly seem to, but what do they mean, do they mean anything different, anything more than my words – and it is your lot, not just you, but the lot of you – why I went to the theatre last week, it was called – called *Chokers*, no, no, it wasn't, *Chancers* it was called, *Chancers*, and it was about these people, people, *what* people, they weren't people, not as I understand the term, they were sex drives, over-articulating sex drives, so that when they said, as they did, 'I'm in love with you', not the slightest twitch of 'in love', the state of being in love crossed the stage, no, it turned out that all they meant is 'I want to fuck you' and when they had the impertinence, no, the *hubris* to utter those most terrifying of words, 'I love you', what did they mean by them? they meant 'I've fucked you and now I need to fuck you again, and possibly a few more times after that and I'll be jealous, insane with jealousy if anyone else fucks you', there are four of them, these Chokers, Chancers, or was it six, anyway, what does it matter how many there were as all they do is fuck each other and all they talk about is how they do it, and who they'd really rather be doing it with or to – and they don't cloak it in their language, they've no use for language as a way of deceiving or purifying once they've made their two declarations, 'I'm in love with you', 'I love you', they're off into their true vocabulary, of cocks and cunts and fuck fuck fucks, no words that even hint at inner lives, no friendships except as opportunities for sexual competition and betrayal, no interests or passions or feelings, as if the man were the cock, the cock the man, the woman the cunt, the cunt the woman, and the only purpose in life to ram cock into cunt, jam cunt over cock, turn and turn about except when they jump the queue and ram and jam when it's not their turn, that's the play, the whole play, and you know – you know the worst thing – the worst thing is that they speak grammatically. They construct sentences. Construct them! And with some elegance. Why? Tell me why? (*Little pause.*) Actually, I know why. So that the verbs and nouns stick out – in your face. In your face. That's the phrase, isn't it? That's the phrase! In your face!

There is a pause. MICHAEL *pours himself another drink.*

MICHAEL. Well, good heavens, I didn't mean – I didn't mean – just an evening at the theatre, after all. Probably quite irrelevant. Can't understand how I got into it.

WENDY. Well, what I can't understand is why you have to use that play and all those words, cocks and cunts and jamming and ramming as a way of not talking about Mum and Japes, and what they did. Because that's what they did, Dad, isn't it, and those are the bits of themselves they did it with, aren't they?

MICHAEL. Your mother and my brother were frequently in love with each other. They loved each other always.

WENDY (*after a pause, laughs*). Oh. Well, that's all right then. Put that way. All purified.

MICHAEL. That way conveys it as accurately as I can.

WENDY. And you knew. Always knew that they loved each other and were frequently in love with each other.

MICHAEL. I understood it, now and then.

WENDY. And you didn't mind?

MICHAEL. Now and then.

WENDY. Well, what about now, as opposed to now and then? Eh, Dad? What do you feel now?

MICHAEL. A sense of completeness. It's run its course, the story. It's over. (*Little pause.*) I talk to them.

WENDY. As a couple? Or individually? And what about?

There is a pause.

WENDY. Oh, sorry, Dad. I shouldn't pry, should I, as it's so sacred. But would you mind telling me so that this one (*Pats womb.*) can know which one's the grandfather and which one's the great uncle. There are rights here somewhere, Dad, aren't there? Probably legal ones, too.

MICHAEL. I don't know. None of us ever knew for sure.

WENDY. And you don't care, do you? What does that sort of thing matter to you lot from the sodding sixties. With your love, love, love and your freedom and flowers and all belonging to each other so what does it matter where the children came from or who they belong to, as long as they're born in love, love, love and the joys of sex, well, it matters to me, Dad, I don't give a fuck about your lot or my lot, but I give a fuck about this one, and our life together, I want to know whether you're my uncle or my father, Dad.

MICHAEL. I was your father, Wendy, in every important respect. In every practical respect. My name was on your birth certificate. And on every cheque that was needed for your provision, and for every institution you attended, from your nursery school to your drugs clinic. Japes was only there for you as an uncle, to give you presents and treats.

WENDY. He was also my best friend. I used to think of him as the only friend I ever had.

MICHAEL. Then he's unlikely to be your father, isn't he? Why should you want him to be?

WENDY. I'm not saying I want him to be. I'm saying I intend to find out.

MICHAEL. Well, I'm sorry, but it seems to me that you'll just have to trust to your instincts. If you want Japes to be your natural father, then have him as such. I'm perfectly happy to remain just your legal one.

WENDY. I'm a long way from the nursery school and the clinic now, Dad. I know what's going on around me, things like DNA, for instance. I'm sure you know all about it too. So you see, Dad, here we are and we want our dues.

MICHAEL. Your dues! I'm not having Japes's body grubbed out of the earth so that you can have your dues, young woman.

WENDY. Oh, don't worry about grubbing Japes up, we don't have to do the test on him, we just do it on you and me. And if you're not the one, then Japes is. Unless there's someone else entirely that we don't know about. Or I'll get a court order. And I can, you know. I've been into it all.

MICHAEL. Really? And on what grounds can a court compel me? I'm not trying to deny that I'm your father. I'm admitting it. Insisting on it.

WENDY. Insisting on it won't make you it, Dad. But that's where our dues come in, you see. Because if Japes is my father, you're not his next of kin, are you, Dad? I am. And everything you got from him belongs to me. Including half this house.

MICHAEL. So that's what you want, is it, half the house? When I've already offered to let you have anything you need – you could have just asked for half the value of the house, if you think you need that much, I'd have found it for you.

WENDY. I don't want half the value, or half the house, I want the whole house, Dad. We'll need the whole of it. This is the only home I've known, and I never got to live in it. Now I want to start life in it again. Our home, I want it to be.

MICHAEL. And you think I'll just give it over to you – the house that belonged to our parents – our childhood home. The only home *I've* ever known.

WENDY. One of the things that's coming around the corner out of the past, Dad, one of the onces, is the 'once upon a time' once. The bedtime story once. It's not clear to me yet, we're working through it, my shrink and I, all we've found out is that there was more than just neglect when I was a child, there was trauma and abuse. There was a bogey-man. One of you was my bedtime bogey-man.

MICHAEL. And will you have me DNA tested for that?

WENDY. My shrink says the way we're working, we'll get to you in the end.

MICHAEL. To me.

WENDY. To one of you.

MICHAEL. I see. And what did this bogey-man get up to, may I ask?

WENDY. Well, as he was a bedtime bogey-man, Dad, it's obvious the kind of thing he got up to, isn't it?

MICHAEL. On the occasions when I put you to bed I read you a Janet and John story. Surely you remember Janet and John? This is Janet. This is John. Hello, Janet. Hello, John. There was one about wellington boots. It was raining but John wouldn't wear his wellington boots. His mother said, 'Wear your wellington boots, John, or your feet will get wet.' His sister Janet said, 'Wear your wellington boots, John, or your feet will get wet.' But John wouldn't wear his wellington boots. 'Silly old wellington boots,' said John. 'I shan't wear them!' Then they all went out into the rain, and soon John said, 'Oh, my feet are wet!' 'I told you so,' said his mother. 'I told you so,' said his sister Janet. So they went home and John put on his wellington boots. Then they went back out into the rain. 'Good old wellington boots,' said John, as he jumped up and down in the puddles. 'Good old wellington boots!'

WENDY (*shakes her head*). Pity I didn't remember it though, years ago. It might have stopped me from getting my feet wet, eh, Dad? No, all I can remember is the bogey-man, his voice saying, 'I am your bogey-man' and chasing me around and around, from corner to corner, and when I got past him and hid in bed he'd come up the stairs, clumping up, one foot clumping after another foot clumping, with gaps in between, long gaps, short gaps, saying over and over again, 'I am your bogey-man, the bogey-man has got you', and I'd be quivering with terror and laughter, both, I'd feel him above me, and I'd feel him bend down, he'd wait. And then – wait. And then he'd whisper 'your bogeyman has got you' and he'd rip the covers right off, and scoop me in his arms. (*Little pause.*) And then when he'd finished with me he'd tuck me in and kiss me on the forehead, and I'd lie there – I'd lie there –

MICHAEL. You'd lie there, would you? It's all a lie – a disgusting lie – and you know it.

WENDY. Yes, I know it, but my shrink doesn't.

There is a little pause.

MICHAEL. There isn't even a shrink, is there? You're just making him up.

WENDY. I'm not making her up. I just haven't got around to choosing her yet. But it won't be a problem, there'll be hundreds and hundreds of them out there just waiting for the chance. And then we can leave it to the court to sort out, though I expect when it comes to it, if Japes turns out to be my real Dad, I'd like you to be the bogey-man, Dad, as I'll already have got everything he's got, so it's best that you're up for the bogey-man damages. I mean, you're the survivor, aren't you, poor old Dad?

There is a pause.

MICHAEL (*almost to himself*). It's not been like this. Not for other generations. Not in my understanding. We didn't start the world, our lot. We didn't come out of nowhere and just – just start you lot off. We were begot, just like you. We were just three people, struggling with ourselves with each other, in our time. Don't you understand? Don't you understand that?

Sound of mobile telephone ringing in WENDY*'s pocket.* MICHAEL *jumps.*

WENDY (*takes mobile telephone out of her pocket, puts it to her ear*). Hi. (*Little pause. Hands mobile to* MICHAEL.) It's Dominic.

MICHAEL. Dominic?

WENDY. Dominic.

MICHAEL (*puts mobile uncertainly to his ear*). Hello? Oh no, not at all, these things happen, I – no, no, really, there's no need – I see, well, right – that's very kind of you – oh, right – (*Hands mobile back to* WENDY.)

WENDY (*taking mobile*). Here I am. (*Little pause.*) We'll talk about it later – (*Little pause.*) all right, you can come over on condition.

MICHAEL *moves towards study.*

But no promises, I don't want any more of your promises, from now on you live by the rules or we do without you, Dommy, it's as simple as that –

Lights beginning to fade.

MICHAEL *exits.*

Yes, of course I know you love us (*Patting stomach.*) and of course we love you – but that's the easy part, anyone can do that, what we've got to do is make it hold together, you see, so that if anything goes wrong, at least we'll know – at least we'll know that we tried, won't we?

Lights.

Curtain.